THE QUIET WATERS BY

PLATE 1

STEELHEAD FISHING, BRITISH COLUMBIA

AYLMER TRYON

The Quiet Waters By

ILLUSTRATED BY
Rodger McPhail

WITH 2 COLOUR PLATES
AND 29 DRAWINGS

H.F. & G. WITHERBY LTD.

First published in 1988 by
H. F. & G. WITHERBY LTD.
14 Henrietta Street,
London WC2E 8QJ

British Library Cataloguing in Publication Data
Tryon, Aylmer
  The quiet waters by.
  1. Angling—Personal observations
  I. Title
  799.1'2'0924

ISBN 0-85493-165-1

Filmset in Monophoto 13pt Apollo
and printed in Great Britain by
BAS Printers Limited,
Over Wallop, Hampshire

To
my great nephew
CHARLES
the keenest of fishermen
who was on one occasion
"cleverer than a trout"

Contents

Illustrations

Colour Plates

Drawings

There are also smaller drawings on pages 3, 5, 6, and 90

THE AVON. A VIEW OF MY NATIVE RIVER

Introduction

I chose the title of this book from the beautiful and restful Scottish metrical psalm, since water has always had a strange attraction for me, perhaps because I was born within a couple of hundred yards of the River Avon, so that no doubt when learning to walk my tottering feet took me down towards the river. I appreciate that not all waters are quiet, but spates all too soon subside. Peace and quiet are indeed synonymous with angling even in this age of mechanical noise, especially so at nightfall when noise abates. As the wise Isaak Walton wrote: *"Piscator. And upon all that are lovers of virtue and dare trust in His providence, and be quiet and go a angling, Study to be Quiet."*

For the last twenty-five years I have lived a mile further down the river in the old mill which I rebuilt and called Kingfisher Mill after one of my neighbours who frequently fishes here, in the company of many water voles, mallard, moorhens and dab-chicks. The river flows quietly through the house with only musical and soporific murmurings, and this week at the end of July, I opened the door of the river room to show a visitor where the mill wheel used to turn when I was a boy, and there was a salmon of about eight pounds swaying in the current below the hatch. A few years ago a salmon of about twelve pounds lay above the hatch. There is much satisfaction in having a salmon in the larder, but much more so in having a live salmon in the house.

My father was a politician and Postmaster General just before the war when they were hoping to re-introduce the penny stamp! When he was asked to speak in another's constituency he would take with him concealed in his case a little four piece rod which he had had made, as he thought his host would suspect his motive for the visit if he arrived with a selection of rods, reels, gaffs and nets! Some said that he was more inclined to speak for those with good fishing, as others did for those with good cellars.

I myself had a gallery in London which specialised in sporting and natural history pictures and so it was essential to travel to different parts of the world in search of artists. If I was inclined to prefer New Zealand, Canada, or even find myself in Patagonia, this tendency was surely hereditary.

This book is not only about fishing but of my visits usually only briefly to those distant lands, and about the wonderful birds and animals that live in or around the rivers and lakes, since water inevitably attracts such creatures to drink and find their food, in the damp meadows or marshes nearby.

This book does not pretend to show how to catch fish in the countries I have visited, since this has been described by abler pens and better fishermen with knowledge of their countries, such as Lee Wulff in America and Roderick Haig-Brown of

British Columbia. The sport and enjoyment of fishing surely lies not only with the numbers of fish nor even their size but the pleasure in being beside these "quiet waters".

I took with me on my travels a strong all-purpose rod of 10 feet built by Hardy's for Steelhead. My other essential was a little pair of binoculars which were given to me many years ago by a kind friend. These survived until last year when I was fishing on the beautiful Tamar River and in order to observe a deep pool more closely where a fish had shown, I knelt on a piece of bank which wasn't there, and did a double backwards somersault from ten feet into the pool below. I did not break any bones nor my rod but ruined my precious binoculars, which had given me almost as much pleasure as my rod, as I hope I will show in the chapters of this book.

I have included naturally some stories of the British Isles and a few anecdotes and incidents often unconnected with fishing; for in the oft-quoted but so true Latin motto of the Flyfishers' Club, freely translated, "There is more to fishing than catching fish".

My friend Rodger McPhail has provided the illustrations as he so kindly did for my previous book *Kingfisher Mill*, and more recently in his own book *Open Season*, drawn from his observations of the Field sports which he loves, understands and records so well with his observant eye and skilful hand.

The Avon

I will start this book with my native river which flowed past my childhood home. My room overlooked the river, towards which the lawns gently slope, set with great cedars and huge spreading plane trees whose tangly branches reach down to the ground. The house is now a girls' school and the children delight in clambering all over these branches which form a natural playroom.

I caught my first fish nearby, so small that I cast again thinking that it was a piece of stick, but at the second cast the poor little grayling shot over my shoulder and was retrieved eventually and carried in triumph to the kitchen. I have lived, whenever possible, in our beautiful village ever since, and I was christened in our fine Norman church.

In 1963 I rebuilt the Old Mill at the southern end of the village, which had become derelict, but I remember from earlier days when the whole building shook as the corn was ground. Now I write in a room with the river flowing beneath, surrounded by birds and animals and indeed fish, all attracted by the food which the river provides. The flies for the fish, swallows, wagtails and warblers; the little fish for kingfishers and dabchicks, and if they survive pursued relentlessly by the grey herons. The swaying river weeds are the home of shrimps, caddis and larvae, and food for my friends the water voles, who sit patiently munching weeds which they often hold in their little paws beneath swaying willow boughs.

Much has changed – to those of us who do not farm, the dreadful sprays have eliminated many of the spring flowers, the flags and king-cups of the jersey-butter yellow are now scarce, although our farmer kindly spares my little meadow where Marsh Orchids and the nodding Water Avens still grow. The Britensis Willows and some of the Weepers are afflicted each year by blight, but the native willows survive.

The Piscatorial Society, who lease much of the river around here, look after the trout and enjoy the kingfishers, voles, dab-chicks and other watery creatures, all of which give pleasure to their members as they stalk their rising fish. Weeds in the river now grow more thickly and more densely, fertilised by the nitrogen sprays washed from the land, but perhaps the water insects and their larvae find more nourishment, and certainly the hatch of flies, and so condition of the fish, has greatly improved. As an example, this mayfly season has been most pro-lific, I counted about a hundred and fifty dead or dying spent mayflies pass within about a yard of the bank in a single minute – an amazing sight – even if fishing was impossible! An hour or so before, the mayflies above the meadows were a shimmering cloud, as if dancing like puppets on gossamer threads.

The Upper Avon too enjoys an almost continuous hatch of small flies throughout the season, so that it is rare to wander up river and not find a rising fish, usually in some awkward place. I am always puzzled as to why a single fish can find so much, whilst others lie quietly on the bottom beneath the unbroken mirrored surface.

My great nephew, Charles, is an ardent fisherman, running in his excitement from rise to rise. Last May a friend saw a good fish rising and called to Charles to fish for it. As the boy approached he heard him say "I am cleverer than you, trout, and I'm going to catch you!" And he did – 2 lbs 12 ozs. My friends and I have been trying these magic words ever since – with no result!

My father enjoyed all kinds of fishing, especially pike, and my great nephew has inherited this preference, so that, should he enter a juvenile Mastermind competition, his specialised sub-ject would undoubtedly be "Poike" as he likes to pronounce the word, as he quotes various leviathans of that troubled isle.

Many years ago my father took me down the river to the Royalty Fishery to try for barbel. We set forth in a punt propelled by the fishery manager, Mr Hayter by name I think. We anchored at the chosen "swim" and I was introduced to the art of ledgering, which I found less exciting than the continuing fascination of watching a colourful float, waiting for it to quiver and then vanish, as the unseen fish at last gives a purposeful tug. Perhaps my great nephew would have some incantation for encouraging a float to disappear too. Now the day was bright and hot and we sat quietly, just feeling the ledger weight straining on the gravel with the current's pulse. I must have almost slept when there was a sudden pull and I struck far too hard and the fish was gone – a most shameful act of an inept and inexperienced fisher. My father, being a most patient and kindly man, merely told me to put on a stronger cast, whilst Mr Hayter too, fearing that I had probably dispersed a shoal of great barbel, offered no reproof. So once more the ledgers and their attendant worms were lowered into the depths of the pool and we sat silently whilst I endeavoured to pay more attention and to keep wide awake. Thus, some time later when there came another pull on my line I tightened more gently and the fish ran strongly out into the current as my reel sang its happy song.

The water was very clear, and Mr Hayter and my father seemed more interested in observing the perch swimming below, ignoring my cries that the fish must be huge. Only when I had manoeuvred the fish closer to the boat and announced that "it must be a salmon" did they suddenly tell me to be more careful, and so eventually Mr Hayter, with a deft twist of the net, lifted the barbel into the boat. The fish weighed 14 lbs 6 ozs and equalled the British record. Beginner's luck and I only wished that my father had caught it, as he deserved to add to his collection of specimen fish, but a most exciting and memorable day for this complete novice.

About the time of the Battle of Britain, we were stationed near Bournemouth, and one day a brother-officer and I took a day's salmon fishing at Somerley. I was well equipped but my friend had no appropriate weapons, so we stopped at a little tackle shop.

PLATE 2

THE QUIET WATERS BY

BARBEL FISHING

There he bought a cheap rod and reel, and we set off for our beat at Ibsley, now the winter haunt of a large flock of the beautiful and melodious Bewicks, and a good number of Whitefronts.

We did not know the beat but started below the handsome stone bridge and thence downstream to a weir. In the afternoon on a bend below this weir, my friend Hugh Burge became attached to some object, so I ran up to investigate. His equipment was most inadequate, being far too light, but at least the object that he had hooked was most animate and played steadily, but the contest showed no sign of being won by either side, whilst I stood by hopefully with my gaff. We had not seen the fish which bored down in a most sullen manner. When we had almost given up hope of a successful outcome, the fish moved up on to some shallower water but was well out from the bank. I could see the position of the fish and so waded out, guided by the line. I could just see the shape and leant forward and managed to gaff it when there was a flurry of spray as I tried to drag it towards the bank. Until this moment we had attributed the length of the struggle more to the lightness of the little rod than to the strength of the fish. However, when we lifted the salmon ashore it weighed 37 lbs and we could then appreciate its fighting power, and admire the previously unpraised qualities of the little rod and reel – a good buy indeed and a great and happy day. We were, for once, the most popular members of our officers' mess that night.

Thus the Avon provides fishermen of all persuasions with wonderful sport. The Upper Avon's chief enemies are pollution and its twin scourge water abstraction. For instance, a thatched boat house, where as boys we would embark in canoe or punt on various forays after pike or eels, is now defunct as it is literally high and dry, some two feet above the water level. The Middle Avon below Salisbury, and indeed as far as the mouth at Mudeford, provides coarse fishing which at one time was probably the best in the country, but has now deteriorated, and the cause is to be the subject for investigation as many suspect effluent from the several huge fish farms. The salmon are large beautiful fish in the springtime, when sadly numbers, as in many rivers, have been in decline. These big fish owe their size to the good feeding in the spawning areas for fry and parr which "smolt" usually after a single year; thus spending an additional year at sea, returning at an average weight of 20 lbs. However, there has been an increased run of grilse and summer fish; and through the efforts of the Wessex Water Authority in providing more and improving fish passes at weirs, salmon are spawning further upstream. Some fish now are seen in the late Autumn, jumping in stretches above my Mill, so perhaps one day I may catch one here, and certainly young Charles will do so if he is also "cleverer than the salmon".

The Frome

Last year we celebrated the fortieth anniversary of our tenancy
of the Bindon Abbey beat of the Frome. My most kind landlords
first let us the fishing for the summer months during the war
when we were stationed nearby, and after the end of the war
we have enjoyed the fishing ever since. As we were gathered
for a celebration party outside the fishing hut a hobby flew low
up the drainage ditch, in search of dragonflies, and banked
steeply away in salute after this fly past. These beautiful little
hawks are my favourite visitors, and at times could be seen
hawking mayflies just in front of the hut, and once I saw a Great
Northern Diver in this same ditch, which dived, caught a little
trout, and surfaced to swallow it. I watched and filmed one in
Iceland which evidently ate his fish under water. The brilliant

amber eyes help his vision as they do for the eagle owl.

After all this time we have had a good many exciting moments; so many dramas around the little bunny bridge above the Mill Pool, that the blank days and sometimes almost blank seasons are soon forgotten. Only last week after a very bleak start a fish rose to my fly so suddenly that I involuntarily lifted my rod and the fish did not forgive.

The little Frome is only ten paces across in some places, I measured it where the railway bridge spans the river, the site of a near fatal accident to a great friend, who was so absorbed dangling a prawn in front of a salmon below, that he failed to hear a train approaching up-wind, and only just threw himself clear as the train passed, so close that a friend fishing below feared that he had been killed. Since then we always fish "facing the engine" and soon will fish there no more, as the line is being electrified.

Although in the spring the Frome runs swiftly and many pools are very deep, my guests are often astonished at its size, and threaten cows on the far bank with their casts. A young friend from the Spey eyed the river with amazement on his first visit, but being most polite, fished away without a word until he reached a pool, appropriately called The Last Hope, where to his great surprise he hooked a fish, which I eventually landed for him. He then looked up and said "Now and only now, do I admit that there really are salmon in this river!"

The Frome spring salmon used to average over 20 lbs but in common with many other rivers, these most sporting of fish are far fewer, although summer fish and grilse are more numerous. Before the war, my predecessors, two brothers, caught six fish in a weekend averaging 29 lbs.

I have so many memories of triumphs, and more often of disasters, that perhaps I may write a little book about these adventures; about the changes that the years have brought, about the birds that come there, as we do ourselves, in the spring migration; about our beloved otters which lived there for most of our time, now for some reason, unseen for the last five years, in an environment seemingly unchanged.

Treble Chance

So I will endeavour to restrict myself to a day which I feel epitomises the variety of fishing which we have been privileged to enjoy. The time of which I write was before the disastrous poisoning of the river from the accidental release of paint stripper from Bovington Camp, which killed almost all the fish from above Wool to the sea. A sickening sight, as fish of all kinds littered the banks and backwaters through this thoughtless act. Fortunately the month was July, so that sufficient salmon had already passed through to ensure a reasonable spawning season, but the few large trout which gave such good sport have vanished, if not for ever, at least for the many years since the disaster. Restocking has failed, probably because these stew fish could not adapt to their new environment, and to a lesser extent because a few voracious pike had survived in the backwaters where there was little flow. Frome pike are huge, one of 27 lbs was caught when electric fishing, with a 5 lb grilse inside! Once weaned on grilse there would seem to be no limit to the size of such salmon swallowers.

Now my errant pen has again wandered from the day I should be describing. The month was May and there was at that time a good hatch of mayfly. One of my ambitions has been to catch a salmon on a mayfly which I have seen them take occasionally, and once watched a fish of about 25 lbs feasting on grannom, as it no doubt had done as a parr. For once I remembered to carry a trout rod with thick cast attached, and so I strolled upstream from the hut, and soon saw the considerable wave of an obviously very large fish rising under the far bank. I walked to a point opposite and as a mayfly floated down it was engulfed by a large mouth, and the ensuing swirl came half way across the river. Trembling with excitement at this long awaited chance, I cast my fly eventually in the right place and watched as it drifted towards the fish, it rose – and of course I struck too soon, or perhaps too late, since I now know that one should strike at once – which should have suited me well. Surely it would rise again? To my horror I saw some cattle wandering slowly upstream on the very edge of the bank, and felt certain that this bovine cavalcade would scare the fish even more than my own efforts had done. When only a few yards short the leading bullock veered away, but still mayfly passed unheeded over the salmon's lie. At last he rose again and I too cast again, but like a disappointed trout refused the fly time and again. So I took off my rejected winged fly and tied on a hackle mayfly and this he took greedily so that he was well hooked, dashed upstream and jumped – about 15 lbs I thought and bright silver. Weeds are a summer's nightmare on the Frome and the fish in a great run upstream swam through a weed bed and thence round a bend above. I managed to clear the line and walked upstream to find that the line led me to a point just above the bend, and I could see the cast pointing down to a hollow beneath. I rolled up my sleeve, lay down and followed with my fingers the gut as far as I could reach, when I suddenly felt the fish itself where the cast had caught on a root beneath the overhanging bank. I perhaps foolishly slid my hand backwards along the fish's side with the vague notion of lifting the fish out by its tail – an impossibility when lying on one's belly, and of course the fish gave a great jerk and the gut broke!

The fish might have been a big sea trout – I caught one of $15\frac{1}{2}$ lbs not long ago on a small salmon fly – but when it jumped I thought it was a salmon, but how strange that it refused the fly again, like a brown trout, a most sagacious creature.

In the afternoon, a little further upstream, I saw another heavy rise but this was obviously that of a sea trout which usually launch themselves thus at the mayflies, perhaps in an attempt to catch them before they take off on their often brief maiden

flights. He was within my range, a fish of about 4 lbs and most
eager to take my fly, and I rose him four or five times, but each
time he, or more probably I missed. I now know that I must
be quick on a salmon with a dryfly, I am well aware that I strike
too late for the graceful grayling rising suddenly from below;
that I am inclined to strike too soon with a large trout, but when
should I strike with such a voracious sea trout?

The third "leg" of my treble chance was a fine brown trout
rising steadily to mayflies and this time I did strike correctly
and the fish did not seek escape in a weed bed and weighed
$3\frac{1}{2}$ lbs. Although this was my only success, I recall those
incidents most vividly of that most memorable day.

Whilst on the subject of the rises of sea trout, I took my
nephew Anthony, when he was a small boy, down to the Mill
at Bindon to try to catch his first sea trout. In the late evening
as darkness began to fade the colours of the landscape, we saw
a fish rising quietly at the tail of the salmon ladder, which we
thought was a good sized brown trout – Anthony was
accustomed to fishing for trout at home and cast his sedge fly
with commendable accuracy just above the fish, which rose and
was hooked. The fish immediately jumped and ran straight down
into the Mill Pool which it investigated at considerable speed.
After several agonising circuits the fish left the pool heading
for the hazardous shallows below, where clutching branches
reach down from the south bank to the surface. The month was
July, tall-growing nettles, grasses, docks, meadow-sweet and
comfrey clutched at the boy's legs and tripped him every few
yards. However, he held his rod aloft whilst I lifted him by his
neck whenever he fell. About a hundred yards below, a deep
carrier joins the main river and at this point, there was no
advance except by swimming. I thought that the contest must
end even if we plunged after him, but the gallant sea trout too
was exhausted, and paused in slack water twixt the main river
and the stream's currents. The light by now had almost gone,
but I could just see the shape of the fish and waded out with

which is even more hazardous for human, and for rod, especially if split cane. The third method was invented by Jonathan Heywood, *faute de mieux*, who in 1986, hooked three fish just above the Mill hatches, which, on each occasion, went straight down into the Mill Pool below. He let them run out much line – he really had little option – and then wedged his rod in a tree, fished up the line in the Mill Pool and played the fish by hand – surprisingly he won twice and lost once – a fish of over 20 lbs, which broke him!

One of the few, if not the only person who negotiated both Bunny and Mill hatches unaided, was Henry Pembroke on 2nd June 1974, who sent a graphic account to the *Field*, which the present editor has kindly allowed me to include.

The battle at the Bunny bridge

. . . Prospects on this day were not startlingly good due to a chronic lack of rain and failure by four other rods even to glimpse a fish on the two previous days. I had, however, purchased some rather anaemic-looking fishmonger's prawns and, scornful though I am of this method of fishing, I felt under the circumstances reasonably justified in taking this action. Unquestionably the best chance of meeting fish is at the 'Bunny'. . . .

The water being low and clear, I could see that the lie above the bridge was empty, but could there be one lurking under the arches? Gently lowering the prawn into the water, I watched it disappear under the bridge. Almost immediately there was a violent tug, followed by some lively splashing.

A considerable efflux of line indicated that the fish had set off downstream and either I would have to follow it through the arch or it would have to come up to me. Deeming the latter to be of more appeal, I tightened on the line and started to wind in. Clearly the fish disagreed with my choice of alternatives and so strong were its objections that I was forced to let it have its own way. As line streamed from the reel I began to think on the first alternative, but while doing so my thoughts were rudely interrupted by the sight of the fish swimming strongly upstream through the further arch.

I saw at once that it was no 30 pounder, nearer 14 I guessed, but it was not failing for strength of purpose. Clearly this present situation could not be allowed to continue, and a make-or-break policy seemed to be the only answer. Clamping both hands firmly on the line, I threw down the challenge.

The fish checked, turned slowly and swam back though the arch (happily the same one). My victory, however, was short lived, for instead of stopping below the bridge as I had hoped it continued on downstream at an alarming rate. The run eventually stopped, but the fish must now be a long way below and I realised that all hope of persuading it to come back was gone.

And so, after all, the rod would have to be transferred to a position below the bridge where I could continue the battle. Once again I had a choice. To accompany the rod under the bridge or to launch it unaccompanied into the water and hope that it would reappear below. Not surprisingly I opted for the latter.

Wedging the rod in the fork of a nearby tree I hooked the line up from below the bridge with the gaff and secured it to the gaff handle. The rod was dropped into the water.

Somewhat to my surprise it came out the other side and I had no trouble in pulling it up. I was now in a position to play the fish, but first to locate it. Its whereabouts justified my worst fears.

It was lying in a small gut, in fast water, just above three hatches through which sweeps the entire weight of the river before shooting off a wide shelf into the mill pool below. It was clear that the fish was poised for retreat through this alarming set of obstacles.

Taking a deep breath I walked slowly downstream hoping I might yet persuade it to swim back upstream. Some hope. Before I had got half way to it an enormous pull on the rod, followed by a screeching of line, told its tale. The fish had made it to the mill pool and if I was going to win I would have to follow it.

The first obstacle then was the hatches, each some $2\frac{1}{2}$ ft wide with only 3 ft of clearance between the water and the wooden planks which topped them. The depth of the water through the hatches was not more than 3 ft and I was confident of negotiating this obstacle without much difficulty. It was, as I found out, a lot harder than it looked.

In the first place the water current was much stronger than I expected, in the second place the river bottom was slippery at this spot, and in the third place I had to depress my 6 ft 3 in frame into dwarf-like proportions in order to get through. With both hands free it would have been hard enough, but with one hand taken up with the rod it was an alarming experience.

After several nervous slips I emerged triumphant below the hatch and clambered up onto the wooden planks. I was wet to the waist but far from beaten. Now I was faced by the biggest obstacle of all. For the shelf, mentioned above, over which the water races before entering the mill pool, is covered at some 4 ft above water level by wire netting. (An obsolete deterrent to poachers, I am told.)

Short of body surfing over the shelf into the pool it was necessary once again to part with the rod. First it seemed wise to check on the fish and, after tightening on the line, I felt, somewhat to my surprise, an answering tug. All was well.

The procedure this time was most complicated. It was necessary, first of all, to hook the line out of the pool, since without it there would be no chance of recovering the rod. After much groping with the gaff in the turbulent water I struck lucky. The line I tied to the gaff and the gaff strap to a sturdy tuft of grass. Now all was ready. I returned to the rod.

Another deep breath, a short prayer to the river Gods, and I gently lowered the rod into the water. At once the racing current swept it over the shelf and into the pool as I dashed back to the gaff, in the hope of seeing it before it disappeared. But already it had sunk out of sight. However, the line was still firmly held around the gaff and all I had to do was pull, and the rod would come up.

And so I started to pull – and I pulled and pulled, and all that appeared was line and more line. The light suddenly dawned. I had forgotten to hitch the line around the reel, thus preventing it from running out. And there was a hundred yards of it on the reel! Despairingly, I lay down on my stomach beside the pool, and stretching out with the gaff, I worked it around under the water with more hope than expectation. Luck had not deserted me. The gaff struck something solid and, on lifting it up, the rod tip suddenly appeared underneath me. I began to scent victory. Grabbing the rod I pulled it out of the water. But there was still one problem to overcome, one which I had created for myself.

Around me lay some forty yards of line. It was caught in the brambles, hooked in branches and tangled in weeds. To unravel it would have taken an eternity. It would surely be easier to cut out the whole shambles and tie the two clear ends together.

Easy enough to do provided the fish did not decide upon this moment to make a run for it. Wherever it was now, it seemed dormant enough and the risk worth taking. Two quick snips, a hurriedly tied knot and the operation was successfully carried out.

Raising the rod, I reeled in the slack line until I felt it tighten. Its resistance over, its battle done, the fish lay close in to the bank at the tail of the pool. There was no difficulty in taking it out.

Its size belied its courage (and its bloody-mindedness). A 13-pounder, fresh and, like all the most stubborn creatures on this earth, a female. The battle had lasted for 50 minutes.

Fish in all rivers are inclined to grow in size, not only after they have been lost, but also after they have been caught, and the Frome is no exception. However this river can claim perhaps the heaviest fish caught in the British Isles on rod and line, albeit by foul hooking, 203 lbs and a kind Dorset fisherman sent me a photograph. This giant fish was a sturgeon and eventually graced a wall of Dorchester Museum for many years. The year was 1911. Whilst there was no need to exaggerate its size, the story of its capture has certainly varied with the passing years.

The story starts with a letter from its captor, Eustace Radclyffe, which was published in the *Field* in May, 1911.

A STURGEON IN THE FROME

Sir, – Whilst I was fishing for salmon in the Frome on May 2 with a companion rod, my friend noticed a fish of remarkable size cruising around on the surface of a pool at Holme Bridge, which is situated some ten miles or more above the river mouth in Poole Harbour. When first seen, at a distance of nearly 200 yards, we pronounced the fish to be a porpoise, but on approaching it more closely, and keeping it under observation for several hours, during which time the fish was on several occasions within 8 or 10 feet of us, upon the surface of the water, we were enabled to see distinctly that it was an enormous sturgeon.

. . . C. E. Radclyffe (Capt.)

A month later he records in his Diary
May 3rd
'I went over with Gibson, but we saw no sign of the sturgeon today . . .'
However on Sunday 2nd July they went over to Bindon, as Radclyffe had heard a sturgeon had been seen there.

The following is an extract from his diary for that day:
'Saw the fish in a big weir pool and tried to catch him with various kinds of baits but all of no use. Then I cast for him with a big salmon fly and managed to foul hook it three times. Raymond and I played it in turns with the rod for about 20 minutes. Twice it broke the line, and once the hooks came out. Finally I sent for a net and we managed to catch it.
The fish (a cock) measured 9 ft $3\frac{1}{2}''$ in length, and $34''$ in girth and weighed just over 200 lbs. I presented it to the King who desired it should be given to a local museum.'
(Actual instructions from Windsor Castle were "... will you kindly preserve and keep same in museum as you suggest ...")
Other sturgeon caught:

Shewsbury	1802	192 lbs	8 ft long
Findhorn	1833	203 lbs	8 ft long
California	1911	270 lbs	8 ft 4″ long

HOBBY HAWKING MAYFLIES

Blagdon

I have so far made no mention of what is now known as "still-water fishing" – a term which annoys me as water is seldom "still". Rivers often run in; the surface is ruffled by wind and the colour of the surface reflects clouds, willows waving in the wind and even rises of trout sometimes break the "stillness". During the war, about the time of the Battle of Britain, we were stationed within reach, even in those petrol-less days, of the beautiful Lake of Blagdon, set high in the Mendip Hills, so well described by Plunket-Greene in *Where the Bright Waters Meet*, "There is not a lovelier sight in England than Blagdon from the Butcombe end at sundown". When we could get leave we would set off in the evenings for this fisherman's haven where a kind lady dispensed tea in the hut overlooking the lake. Blagdon is a reservoir of the Bristol Waterworks Company, to which the great Lake of Chew has since been added. Except for the dam at one end Blagdon has an entirely natural appearance. The reed beds are the "haunts of coot and hern" and in winter of wildfowl of great variety, especially wigeon, teal and mallard, with diving ducks in the deeper pools. Many elegant Great Crested Grebes nest there with their colourful spring bonnets, and I remember a party of Black Terns drifting by as they fished in the shallows; and many varieties of waders.

The fishing interests were looked after by a delightful Scotsman named Angus. Because at that time there was thought to be a risk of gliders, sea planes or other air borne carriers landing on the water, poles had been erected, and a curfew imposed at dusk. The Home Guard took over at night and as there was really no threat of anything landing except spinners, they usually settled comfortably in the hut provided for them and the windows soon steamed up. We would then retire to the more remote bays to await the evening rise, to watch for the cruising fish, and

29

many were very large – both Brown and Rainbow trout – and to enjoy the peaceful Somerset scene as the light faded.

Then would the large fish move into the shallows on the reed beds' edge to chase fry venturing forth from their daylight hide-away, and hatching sedges, dragonfly nymphs and lesser flies.

We would wade out and try to anticipate the trout's erratic course. Sometimes I would try one of the deep ditches or the inflow stream at the top, letting the fly sink and hoping to see a dark shape emerge from the tree roots. I avoided the dam at the end, preferring the more natural scenery at the shallower upper end. There was something rather magical about those still Blagdon evenings. The silence of the night was only broken by flighting duck, and the "plop" of a rising fish or by the screech of a reel as a fish took, followed, if the trout escaped, by the soon stifled oaths of the luckless fisherman, echoing across the lake, where sound carries such distances. Angus was well aware of our activities and turned the proverbial blind eye, and deaf ear as well.

One evening we heard that the General Manager of the Bristol Waterworks was coming over and in order to show our appreciation of Angus, we agreed for once to return to the hut at the appointed hour and so went off to our favourite fishing haunts.

I was the first to return but as darkness curtained the lake, and as the curfew hour had long passed, I sat fuming in the hut – that my brother officers and brothers of the angle could be so uncharacteristically false. At last they walked cheerfully in, proudly and unashamedly displaying their catch.

When I remonstrated they said "Oh, didn't you hear that the charming Manager had told Angus that we could fish for as long as we liked"!

In those sad and anxious days, when enemy formations on their way to destroy Bristol were seen on their deadly flight paths, with many aerial battles, and with the dull distant thud of exploding bombs, and the eerie wail of sirens, fishing – which is the best antidote in troubled times – provided much solace.

E WILD SPRING CALL OF THE CURLEW

Scotland

Scotland has held a special place in my fishing affections ever since I first travelled North on the night train to wake in wonderment in the midst of heathery hills and saw there my first view of red deer and grouse, and the rocky pools of rivers and little burns. On my arrival after a huge breakfast in the dining car, I was soon to meet other companions of those northern rivers and rocks, the ever-curtseying dippers, the delightful red-nosed oyster catchers, which are there mostly mussel catchers, and heard for the first time the wild call of the curlew's tremulous spring song, a reminder whenever heard of that beautiful strath of Helmsdale.

Scotland has so much to offer, such varieties of rivers and lochs from the great salmon rivers to humble burns; from the silver fresh run salmon and sporting sea trout, to the many wild trout of the myriad lochs; and even the ancient colourful char of some high lochs. All these have an important essential in common, that our catch, if landed, will be delicious to eat especially if fried or grilled in oatmeal.

The Helmsdale

My introduction to salmon fishing came from Miss Ratcliffe, a dear old lady who asked me to stay for a week in 1925. I could not have had a better tutor nor a more beautiful river for my initiation. I must have been most inept since my last day arrived and I had still caught nothing. My charming and patient ghillie who must really have been exasperated by my feeble efforts eventually took the rod and hooked a fish, which I played but of course it did not count as my first salmon.

In spite of my failure my hostess, who should have been elected a Saint, asked me to stay again the next season, and so I went up by the night train in a fever of anticipation, and eventually caught my first salmon. But this was not the only exciting event since the year was 1926. I was wearing my best Sunday suit for the journey South sitting in front of a framed notice which read "I would it were a'coming ye were and na a'going", whilst I ate my final breakfast. Soon this prayer was miraculously answered by the timely arrival of a telegram from the station master at Inverness which read "Strike expected midnight – advise not travel". I changed back into comfortable clothes and was fishing again within half an hour. There was an Admiral fishing also on the river. He had to re-join his ship and decided to hire a car to drive South. Hearing that I was also unable to get South and with unusual lack of tact for a sailor, he called on Miss Ratcliffe to offer me a lift. The Admiral went South alone!

Those who have fished this delightful river will know that the railway line runs up the Strath parallel to the river. After about a week, a train manned by an amateur crew, mostly I think undergraduates, could be heard puffing and hooting as if Casey Jones himself was at the throttle of his six-eight wheeler on his way to 'Frisco.*

The train returned somewhat vaguely the following day, or perhaps the day after. On each day if the beat, which changes each day, was sufficiently near, Miss Ratcliffe would send her ghillie, Willie Bannerman, to carry a fish up onto the track and hold it aloft. The driver would then do his best to stop the train, when the fish would be handed up for the benefit of the gallant crew. Tooting its thanks the train would then puff its way up the strath.

All this was magic to a small boy and whenever I hear the haunting spring cry of the curlew, or see golden plover in their spring plumage as I did in Iceland, I am reminded of my pro-longed holiday and the peat fire of the Lodge of Kildonan and especially of my kind hostess.

She had an ambition to catch a 30 lb fish – very rare on that

---

*'Casey Jones' was a celebrated American Railroad song with a splendid rhythm. Casey was a 'brave engineer' who won fame on a six-eight wheeler when he "mounted to the cabin with his orders in his hand, and took his farewell trip to that promised land."

> Put in your water and shovel in your coal,
> put your head out the window watch them drivers roll
> I'll run her till she leaves the rail
> cause I'm eight hours late with that Western Mail.
>
> Turned to the Fireman, said Boy you'd better jump
> 'cause there's two locomotives thats a'going to bump

(the end)
> Mrs Jones sat on her bed a-sighing
> just received a message that Casey was dying
> Said 'Go to bed children, and hush your crying
> 'cause you got another papa on the Salt Lake Line.'

river, but one day as she ate her "piece" she told Willie to fish and he hooked and landed such a salmon. "What did you do with it?" a friend asked her – "Ach" she said in disgust, "I SOLD it!" I truly believe that this was the only fish she ever sold, such was her generosity. I often think of this when I hear fisherman boasting of large catches and the price they have received for their salmon. We have much to learn from Americans in this respect. However I have a remedy and when a jealous or boastful fisherman tells me that he has caught a dozen fish in a day, I reply "Oh! What went wrong?" in grateful memory of Miss Ratcliffe!

A small burn in Angus

Invermark lies at the head of Glen Esk, a wonderful sporting estate to which the Laird has most kindly asked me on many occasions. But on the occasion of which I write, my host was an American friend.

We were driving grouse and on this particular day on the beat beyond Loch Lea which lies just above the Lodge – a fine high moor with many deer as well as grouse. When we reached the Lea stables, a couple of miles beyond the head of the loch, the mist was down so we wandered around restlessly saying that the mist would surely lift, and that some tree had not been visible a minute before. After about an hour I conceived the idea of trying to catch some burn trout from the little burn which might be called the water of Lea but the name matters not at all. I found a length of string and some horse hairs borrowed from the pannier ponies in the stables and attached these to the end of my cromach or long stick, meant for stalking. Luckily, I had as usual some flies under the lapel of my coat, and half cast or dangled a fly into the little burn which was in good order.

Now most of the Americans were members of the Anglers Club of New York, a diminutive building on Wall Street flanked by great sky-scrapers. I lent them in turn my improvised rod and, although used to the Restigouche, Moisie and Grand Romaine,

THE SMALL BURN

they fished even more keenly than if they were on those great rivers, crawling to the edge and shouting with excitement as they rose or hooked a fish. Somehow, I seem to remember that on several occasions the fly was cunningly concealed by a worm, the traditional bait of small boys fishing small burns in spate. We had quite forgotten about the mist when the call to arms was suddenly announced.

''TIS AN ILL WIND . . .''

Spey

The third episode occurred on the noble Spey at Knockando where the river is flanked by beeches with firs above and the pools succeed one another, each as enticing as the last to fish and to fishers, which include the possibility in late evenings of seeing the flat head of an otter and certainly a graceful roe.

I remember the evening of which I write was the first day of September, following a day of gales. The keeper had told me that a few duck were flighting to a corn field and as this was the first day of the season I promised to meet him there.

I was fishing the Long pool with the head ghillie, Sandy. This pool, as the name implies, is long and shallow, and eventually glides into a very deep hole beneath a rock on the right bank. From this hole as the light fades salmon emerge and swim slowly up to the neck of the pool and beyond, returning before dawn to their diurnal fastness. This most exciting half hour is followed by a rise of sea trout which for some reason seem to prefer darkness.

On this particular evening I suddenly noticed fish rising at the tail of the pool as if they were trout being fed in a hatchery. So we dropped down in the boat to investigate and saw that they were a shoal of salmon rising at the many leaves floating down after the day's gale.

In that year I had never caught a salmon on a dry fly, but my small rod and dry flies were at the hut at the top of the pool and there was no time to go up there. So I held my salmon rod aloft and dapped a small fly on a very short line over any fish which showed and some were very close to the boat. I did succeed in catching a couple and in losing others, and then we had to leave to keep my rendezvous with Walter the keeper, arriving just in time to shoot a few duck for dinner. I asked Sandy if he had ever before seen salmon rising to leaves. He replied that whilst he himself had not, his father had told him that he had once watched a similar scene on the Deveron. Salmon fishing has many dull periods but is full of revelations such as these salmon at play.

On the same visit in the "draw" of the pool Vrennan accompanied by Jimmy Gray – a great Spey-caster and now superintendent of the Spey District Board – the day being hot and bright, I decided to try a dry fly. Jimmy was fascinated by the prospect and volunteered to cross in the boat and to climb out along the branch of an overhanging oak beneath which a good fish had been showing. When he was in position I waded out and cast a large bumbly dry fly so that it drifted down over the fish which Jimmy could clearly see. At last the fish rose slowly with open mouth, but Jimmy in his excitement shouted "he's coming to it" – alas I too was so over-excited that I struck before the fish had reached the surface, whilst Jimmy nearly fell from his precarious perch on to the frustrated fish below!

I have recently returned from another most enjoyable if unproductive autumnal visit to Spey and Tay. The former full of fish which wouldn't take, the latter more restful and less frustrating with very few fish, due to over-netting.

My dog Drake was featured prominently in *Kingfisher Mill* as runner-up in "The Worst dog in Wiltshire" Trial. He dislikes fishing except where rabbits or moor-hens abound, but thinks that he should be mentioned in this book.

So when my hostess on the Spey reported a rabbit in her beautiful and immaculate rose beds, which are framed by a beech hedge some four feet high, I hunted Drake through the roses, but drew blank, and then suddenly espied a rabbit outside a clump of shrubs about the length of a cricket pitch from a gap in the hedge. The rabbit's head was raised so I stalked silently behind the hedge, and as we reached the gap and before I could say "hey lost" Drake saw the rabbit, covered the distance in even time and bowled the rabbit over. Unfortunately the rabbit was made of stone and my hostess had possessed him since a child.

Luckily when I visited the wonderful Baxter's establishment the following day, I saw a splendid ceramic rabbit decorated with flowers, which Drake sent to our hostess with his apologies.

My visits to both these great rivers were enhanced by the unmistakeable sight of the "hover" of ospreys. Being heavy birds they lack the grace of the Kestrel or "Windhover" as they are sometimes aptly called, now so often seen over the fringes of motorways, where so much wildlife flourishes. The hover of the osprey seems to me to resemble a strange medallion hanging from the sky by invisible thread; upright in poise, with head thrust forward, the stiff primaries extended at right angles. I am reminded each time of an osprey which fished here for five weeks in October, and others seen fleetingly since then. Will another fish here this autumn on its unhurried journey south, as I await the return of my water rails from Scandinavia?

ROW, BROTHERS, ROW, THE STREAM RUNS FAST,
THE RAPIDS ARE NEAR AND THE DAYLIGHT'S PAST . . .

(*Canadian Boating Song*)

The Mighty Tay and little 'Moorhen'.

Some friends and I rented the prolific Islamouth beat of the Tay for a week one autumn. John Ashley-Cooper used to take up on the roof of his diminutive car, a little fibre glass boat named *Moorhen*, to supplement the large sturdy Tay boat provided.

The river on this occasion was high and I was given strict instructions as to where I should drop anchor in a certain pool. This I did to the best of my ability, but I always preferred cricket to rowing so that I was never very skilled in a boat. The anchor immediately began to drag until catching firmly on a rock far too near the "draw", above a steep and very rocky rapid. Whilst I was considering this quandary a fish took my fly – one of the few occasions when such an event was not welcome. The fish was only a grilse but when I eventually dragged it alongside I managed only to gaff the gut and in such a small boat there was no room to manoeuvre. At that moment John appeared on the bank above, watched for a few moments, considered the situation "absolutely hopeless" and walked sadly away, upstream, mourning no doubt the inevitable loss of his precious boat and incompetent friend.

THE FIBRE GLASS "MOORHEN" AT THE POINT OF NO RETURN

By hand-lining I eventually got the fish aboard but was then faced with the problem of upping the anchor and avoiding the clutches of the rapids. In such a light boat water shipped over the bows as soon as I pulled on the anchor chain, so that when eventually, with a final heave, the anchor came aboard, the craft was even more unstable. I jumped to the oars by which time *Moorhen* hung precariously above the rapids. I rowed frantically keeping one eye on a tree alongside. For a few moments we remained level and then the tree began to gain and went upstream whilst I decided to go down the rapids stern-first, having really no alternative. When a rock loomed up astern, I heaved on the appropriate oar and thus arrived safely if breathlessly in the pool below to the astonishment of Patrick Hazlehurst who was fishing there.

When John appeared later I told him that I would have been happier if he had walked away downstream, when at least he might have gaffed me! I was reminded of the story of the Scottish Ghillie when the fisherman waded too deep and was carried away downstream. When he clambered out far below, he returned in anger to the ghillie who said "Well Soor, I canna swim and I didna' want to see ya drown so I turned ma back and lit ma pipe"!

John himself was an intrepid wader and once rescued a friend on the Spey who had reached a point of no return and no advance, by wading in from the far side, linking arms and conveying him safely and thankfully ashore. He was always willing to give advice from his knowledge of those great rivers, and was only dangerous when driving his little car packed with huge rods, veering to point out a pool on the Tay where Miss Ballantine had caught her record fish, or other points of interest.

Sea trout in the Isle of Skye

My first introduction to these most sporting fish was on the estate of Strathaird on the southern shores of this most beautiful isle. Haunting in every sense of the word, and often wet as well as misty. At the kind invitation of my friends the three Johnson brothers who at that time owned this magnificent estate in the Cuillin hills, I fished there for many years and well remember my first visit to the house at Kilmarie, where hung many Chinese paintings of fascinating scenes, and of birds and beasts. The little river there was in spate when I arrived, and I was astonished when we went out after tea to find that the river was already too low to fish!

The following day we walked over to Camasunary, an hour's walk or ride on fat hill ponies, or otherwise a longer journey by sea. I remember well my first view of the magical bay, with the lodge almost "set in a silvery sea" with only the sands between. And there in the bay, as if huge stones were being thrown, were splashes which I soon saw were shoals of sea trout. So abandoning the zig-zag pony path I ran straight down the steep hill face and was soon casting over the fish which I could see as the waves of the incoming tide lifted the sea weed patches where the fish were lurking. The response was as so often when hopes are high, most disappointing; their reaction was an occasional half hearted wave as they followed the fly, and seldom a perfect rise as in loch or river. But one Saturday night I did hook a good fish from a boat which took us well out into the bay. My host asked Lachy, the ghillie, whether he had feared that the hour of the Sabbath would have arrived before we landed the fish, to which he replied that he thought that we would not net it until Monday! The fish was about 6 lbs.

The loch of Coruisk lay concealed in the heart of the Cuillins about half an hour by boat with outboard motor, or on one occasion when these uncertain machines failed, at least an exhausting hour's row with a young and very strong ghillie at the other oar.

On the occasion of which I write the loch was still, which is ideal for that loch. Our outboard worked perfectly and our wake was illuminated by tiny phosphorescent stars which were

LOCH CORUISK

some form of crustacea. We landed and followed the short river up which fish can only pass on the spring tides or in heavy spate. The view of the loch is surely one of the finest spectacles in Scotland, with the high Cuillins rising almost vertically, and at night so awe-inspiring that one speaks quietly as though entering a great natural cathedral. We paused and sat in silence, partly in admiration, and to await the coming of darkness before rowing to the shallow head of the loch, where a gentle river flowed from a great corrie over a black patch, the haunt of the loch's large sea trout at night.

The month was June so darkness was slow to come and the loch was strangely silent as the moon rose. We rowed quietly up the loch and suddenly were startled by cries as nesting gulls and terns protested at these nocturnal intruders so close to their young as we passed an island. At last we reached the head of the loch.

Now was the great moment come, and we cast on either side of the boat. Sea trout at night take most gently until hooked when the mirrored surface broke like some shattered great plate glass window, as these athletic and beautiful fish jumped, fell back, and jumped again. The creaking of our rowlocks too broke the silence in an almost discordant noise on so magical a night. For this was, for once, a time when everything exceeded expectations. Some were "moonies" as we called fish of 8 lbs or more – a name mistakenly derived from a gaelic expression used by our ghillie. We caught I believe fifteen fish weighing seventy-three pounds, five over eight pounds, on that memorable night of nights and returned happily home as dawn etched again the outlines of shore and indeed the Cuillin hills themselves. We ate delicious finnock, the best of all breakfasts, and with a much needed dram of whisky, surely the perfect end to a perfect night, on this my favourite loch where the Golden Eagles often soar by day, blending so perfectly with their natural surroundings. May they long survive.

"The Skye Boat Song"

Writing of Skye I was reminded of one occasion at the end of a week, when my kind and generous host invited the Glen Pipe band to play before and during dinner.

The band duly appeared in their smartest dress, some wearing the kilt, and marched up and down the lawn, playing appropriate Highland airs with some skill. All went well until, as we were about to go into dinner, our host, who was stone deaf, waved his arm towards the drink tray saying "Help yourselves".

Now a bottle of whisky had been placed for them on the tray, which also held bottles of Martini of various brands and in those days of cocktails, a splendid assortment of vodka, gin, brandy, Cointreau and other delights. We then trooped into dinner.

After about half an hour the gallant band began to play again, but it was apparent to all but our host, that all was not entirely well with the music. As they refilled their glasses, so did the pipe music become wilder and more difficult to recognise. When we at dinner reached the port and dessert stage, the pipe band most unsteadily embarked on the boat to Skye which misty isle it would have been unlikely to reach if our splendid crew were at the oars. Indeed the only way we could recognise that haunting tune was through the efforts of the youngest member of the band who was not allowed to drink anything except lemonade, and thus the clear notes from his flute continued to convey the Bonny Prince when others had long since sunk without trace.

As we returned to the drawing room we were most apprehensive lest our host should take offence and not least that the splendid members of the band through a mistaken signal, worthy of Nelson, should feel that they had abused his hospitality.

As we entered the room the gallant pipe major stood framed in the open French windows and said with a slight bow, "Thank ye verra much sooor" and as the host turned away into the room, over corrected the bow and fell backwards down the steep wooden steps into the garden below to join the other, already prostrate members of his band. Even this final crash went unnoticed and unheard.

Long after midnight an attempt was made to drive their bus down the Glen. Unfortunately the "wee laddie" had not learnt to drive, and a volunteer after threatening several silver birches with destruction soon gave up the idea. Thus they slept until woken by "the grey dawn breaking" by which time the most gallant Pipe major was fully in charge, as the 'bus clattered down the glen, each member of the band being ejected as the 'bus passed his door. A memorable and happy end.

Eire

The Blackwater

I was most fortunate to be invited for many years to Careysville, at first by a friend of my father's and then by the Proprietor. In the first few years Lionel Richardson from Waterford was one of the rods. He was the "king" of the Daffodil growers, winning the gold medal each year at the R.H.S. spring show. When he died, his widow very kindly sent me a huge sack of bulbs when I was starting a garden at my Kingfisher Mill. These wonderful varieties have increased each year and are a constant reminder each spring of Lionel and our happy times at Careysville.

The house overlooks the river with the great weir above and fast water below, culminating in wide slower reaches known as The Flats. These were clearly visible from my bathroom window, and although memory tends to exaggerate, I counted over a hundred fish jump, or perhaps jumps, in five minutes – or was it only a minute? This made shaving difficult and painful, and one cold February day my sponge was frozen! The remedy as with ice in the rings was to dip the rod (or sponge) into the water. Fishing in early February was mainly with heavy minnows, as the tradition was that a fly was useless before St. Patrick's day, but we did surprise the Saint at times with a few fish on the fly.

Billy Flynn, the celebrated ghillie and teller of tales, was usually allotted to me as some rods found his oft repeated stories distracting. My own favourite of many, was the first salmon proven to have fed in fresh water. The rod concerned had offered Billy a £5 note if he succeeded in catching a fish of 30 lbs, and a few days later he hooked and landed a fish that Billy thought might be of such weight. So he carried it up to the house and into the kitchen where it was put on the scales, which to his chagrin would register only $29\frac{1}{2}$ lbs. Happily at this moment the remains of the lunch were brought in, and so Billy, when cook's back was turned, shoved a generous helping of cake and cheese down its throat. Yet still the weight was a couple of ounces below the desired mark. So an orange was added to the feast and then Billy rushed down to the river below announcing that the fish weighed exactly 30 lbs and was duly rewarded by the delighted angler.

After some days a letter was received from the Minister of Fisheries himself, to say that one of his Inspectors at Billingsgate had noticed a fine salmon with a very distended stomach so he had opened it up only to discover that it had eaten fruit cake, cheese and an orange, and was the first really authenticated instance of a salmon feeding in fresh water!

I caught my largest salmon with Billy which needed no such additions. I was fishing a pool called the Top Flat just below the weir, and hooked this fish which was very strong, and the pool is full of hazards and needs agility to follow if the fish decides to go down. Now Billy, although he had gaffed hundreds of fish, became very over-excited if the fish was large, and was inclined to slash at it in the manner of someone like myself trying to get out of a deep bunker. So it was customary to exchange rod for gaff. When we eventually landed the fish there was a great cheer from the opposite bank as if we had just scored a goal. We looked up in surprise, to find that all the workers from the Mill opposite had come out to watch the contest.

Whilst all rivers have characters of their own some seem to have personalities which appeal to individual fishermen. Whilst my own personal preference is for the smaller, faster rivers, yet I must confess that the Irish Blackwater has a quite extraordinary appeal, an atmosphere which is unaccountable, like the invisible power which causes the diviner's hazel wand to thrust upwards as he crosses a water course below ground; or as some can feel on entering a haunted house. Perhaps the Irish blarney is responsible, certainly it is part of the charm.

At Careysville the very names of the pools are an example and have the celtic lilt – Likanans or the Coleneen; the endless Irish stories of which one of my favourites occurred just below Careysville just after the war, when a fisherman was looking for a house to buy in the district. He had heard that such a place was for sale on the north side of the river, and wanting to know details of the house, turned to his ghillie, who confirmed that it was "a foine house" but on being asked whether it had a long drive replied, "Indeed it has Sorr, but if it was any shorter it wouldn't reach the house"!

I have a strong preference for fishing a fly later in the season, especially with the floating line, but fishing the wide "flats" where many fish congregated at times, with large heavy minnows, casting without the assistance of the too easy modern thread-line reels, was most exciting, with many "over-runs". We fished our minnows slowly and deep, but when once a friend on the other bank caught the bottom, I tried to release the bait by catching his line. When I missed I wound in as fast as possible and a fish took, half way across – typical of our sport!

Billy Flynn insisted that a strange bait known as a leather eel, was the best bait in the late evening. I later discovered that his preference was because it was an inconspicuous and heavy weight, and the fish couldn't see it coming! He said that fish "hooked outside" played better.

Careysville possesses the most excellent and my favourite fishing hut, where, through the kindness of the owner – the most generous and hospitable of men – a stove was lit to dry our wet clothes, a much needed hot meal, and most plentiful supply of warming drinks were provided to restore our circulation as we told, with increasing inaccuracies our adventures of the morning. Whilst on the lawn outside – graced later in the year by many daffodils – lay the morning's catch, to be admired for their invariable freshness, as befits these beautiful silver fish, often adorned with the tide lice. Perhaps our total catch might have been greater if we had not dallied for so long, but certainly our enjoyment would have been no greater, and on all rivers the time spent in the hut, could be a gauge to the probability of success. I remember a book devoted most seriously to the taking times of salmon, in which the Author appeared to be puzzled by the few fish caught between one and two o'clock. Fishing should never be too serious, we are beside our beloved rivers to enjoy ourselves, and we do!

The house at Careysville, as I have said, stands high above the river, and at one time a donkey cart brought the lunch down to the hut, returning later in the day with the fish, which in those days were numerous. Later a steel hawser with basket attached took the place of the donkey, less romantic, but perhaps on good days, less exhausting for Neddy. A charming artist, who sadly died recently, told me that she wanted to paint the familiar scene of a donkey cart with milk churn, arriving at the creamery. So she waited and watched a man up a ladder, painting the gutter. At last, down the lane came a donkey cart. The farmer dismounted, tied his donkey to the bottom of the ladder, and carried his churn within. She said that she had never seen even a fireman descend a ladder more swiftly than the painter.

The great weir was the scene of another of Billy Flynn's stories. A telegram arrived for the Duke, who was fishing the Top Flat and was taken over by boat. Billy was the ghillie on the house side, so, the Duke, after reading the telegram, shouted across to ask him to go up to the house to tell cook that there would be five for dinner instead of three. The noise of water always deadens other sounds, and the weir pool was deafening. So Billy went up to the kitchen and said to the Cook "Grace says there will be pie for dinner instead of tea". The cook, thinking that the Duke had gone mad, since they were not having pie anyway, sent Billy back to the river to enquire what pie he would like. The Duke, by then as confused as any, shouted back "Magpie of course" and mercifully that was the end of this improbable tale.

One year the river was very low, and so we persuaded Billy to ask the priest, at mass, to pray for rain. When he joined us after lunch, we asked if he had done so. "Oh yes" he replied but the priest said "No Billy, I will not whilst the wind remains in the East."

I still have memories of his tall lean figure striding up and down the bank, and of his usual morning greeting – "The river is in perfect order and there are hundreds of fish, mad with hunger, jumping all over the river!" Laughter followed wherever he went, so good for our morale and indeed, such a ghillie is a joy to be with. I abhor the dour gloomy ghillie to whom nothing is ever right.

*　　*　　*

There is nothing more frustrating for eager fishers on a short holiday than to wake to a wet dawn when drawn curtains reveal that the water below is indeed black and obviously rising. So we assembled for breakfast at Lismore in unusual gloomy silence as we sadly munched our delicious kedgeree – the nearest we were likely to get to one of those noble fish for at least a couple of days.

We decided at once not to go up the fifteen miles to Careysville, since to watch a rising river, sticking twigs at the river's edge which are instantly engulfed, is one of the worst afflictions known to fishing men. On a previous occasion, I remember, we had sought solace at the local point-to-point. This turned out to be a hilarious experience straight from the pages of Somerville and Ross.

The course was as water-logged as our river, the going heavy. There was a splendid Master of Ceremonies clad in a much-needed long mackintosh, mounted on an agile hack. Before the start of a race he could be seen riding frantically to the overflowing beer tent, scattering the crowd and their numerous dogs, and screaming at those riders in the next race to get mounted, as they downed yet another confidence-booster. Our hero, having assessed their capabilities and especially their incapabilities, then rode swiftly to the nearest bookie and thence to the start where most of the participants were by then assembled. As soon as his selection was facing the right way, he called out as if one word 'are-ye-ready-then-away-weth-ye'. Snipe rose as the runners approached one of the several banks which were such hazardous obstacles in those early days, and some spectators belaboured their tiring selections with their staves as they clambered onto the bank.

The Master of Ceremonies, having judged the first horse past the post, then rode to the scales and announced through a megaphone 'winner all right – Glenpatrick' for such was indeed the name, and we hoped that our character had, as we suspected, been duly rewarded.

So our day of frustration ended in sharing the enjoyment which only the Irish could conjure from this truly sporting occasion.

But to return to Lismore. Our host suddenly remembered that the woodcock season overlapped for a few days with the salmon; so a local worthy, who was rather lame, was despatched to find men and dogs to beat the glen, and such sporting occasion in Ireland is never short of volunteers.

The glen which we were to shoot consisted of a fast-flowing but shallow river with steep wooded and bramble-clad sides. A wall about four feet high prevented the river from flooding the road and inebriated motorists from driving into it. By then some ten beaters had been assembled, together with two terriers, a fierce-looking mongrel named Ebenezer who was said to bite, and a fat and quite useless spaniel – so unlike most of that noble breed.

The head beater hobbled up the centre of the road which for some reason he tapped vigorously, whilst the remainder spread themselves up the right-hand side. The guns walked in line ahead up the road about forty paces apart. Irish beaters with their enthusiasm and cries add enormously to the excitement, whilst the 'cock themselves in such wild country swerve and dive with amazing speed and even with one's own gun are very difficult to shoot, and delicious to eat.

Our line of beaters uttered a musical chant as they progressed with difficulty through the thick tangly undergrowth, 'fly away 'cock, fly away 'cock, fly away!' When a 'cock rose there was an excited scream 'to the right' often regardless of the actual direction, but the 'cock from the higher side would often cross the valley, very sporting shots, whilst others would dive low at the guns in most elusive fashion.

If a bird was shot it almost invariably fell into the flooded stream, when the gun concerned would put down his gun, race down the road until he judged that he was ahead of the bird, vault over the wall and plunge into the river, there taking stance, as in the slips, and field the bird as it swept past; only to repeat the whole process, if he missed, whilst the panting beaters recovered their breath.

My host tells me that we shot a dozen 'cock on that memorable non-fishing day, and beaters, yapping dogs and guns returned soaked, exhausted and very happy to quench enormous thirsts and await, like Noah, the abatement of the flood.

FIELDING THE WOODCOCK

Iceland

When asked where I have enjoyed the finest salmon fishing I say Iceland with little hesitation; whilst Norway scenically and for weight of fish, and the waters in which they live, are in my experience unsurpassed. I confess that I have never fished any of the great Canadian rivers.

My preference for Iceland stems from my enjoyment of fishing small clear streams with a ten foot rod, where one can often see and watch the fish and try different methods at suitable times. Iceland too has great varieties of my favourite birds most of which are very tame in the breeding season, and also many wild flowers which have belatedly interested me. The fish too are such good takers and if you see a salmon jump he will more often than not at least rise at your fly, so that when next you fish in Scotland and see many fish show in a pool you are very soon deflated when none take. The Icelandic fish too are evidently not far from their feeding grounds and still retain their feeding teeth which gashed fingers will soon testify. When hooked they are incredibly strong and if they decide to leave the pool you must run over the boulders like a demented goat and try to arrive at the next with some backing left on the reel and some breath left in the lungs.

The Haffjardara

I have fished only two such rivers in Iceland. So may I first describe the Haffjardara, a little river in the south-west with a lake at the top with an artificial narrow outflow – obviously the former site of a fish trap – with a lava field on the left bank full of voracious mink, and at times the resting place of the white-tailed eagles which sit motionless on top of pinnacles in heraldic

53

pose as if carved from the lava rock. Below the outflow is a narrow lake and thence the river tumbles steeply in a series of pools for some couple of miles, no larger than a big burn in Scotland. Below this there are a series of flat wide pools full of fish often in shoals awaiting a spate for the hazardous ascent to the lake.

There are few salmon pools which are indeed "absolute certainties" but such was the outflow. There were only two problems, one how to reach the bank on the lava field side from which the run could best be fished, the other was the mink. The first year we waded across the shallows at the end of the narrow lower lake and thence set off on a nightmare journey through the lava field which consisted of crumbling rocks with quite deep little valleys. Keeping direction was very difficult and only achieved by climbing little pinnacles which often gave way. We all suffered from wounds which because of the lava dust refused to heal. The return journey was even more hazardous as the weight of salmon often caused painful falls and I once broke my rod – if one had broken a leg in one of the deep lava bowls discovery and indeed recovery would have been difficult. However the journey was always well worth while, and later a much longer route mostly along the lake shore was found to be safer and quicker. The last year I bought and carried up a small inflatable rubber dinghy. The idea was to attach a cord to a rock and throw it across the narrow gap and then pull the dinghy and myself across. This worked well when outward bound but on the return, laden with a few salmon, the wind had risen blowing the waters at some speed through the gap. Furthermore the little craft had become deflated due to a leak, so that when I climbed aboard and sat down I was enveloped like a cloak and in mid-channel the rock decided to leap off the wall so that I was anchored firmly in mid-stream. Luckily by paddling with the bailer I just managed to reach shore before we sank with all fish and rod – oars were too cumbersome to carry.

The mink had established a stronghold at the outflow where

MERLIN AND PIPIT

tecting their young against these foreign fishers. I found difficulty in casting and especially in playing fish whilst avoiding
their attacks, as they knocked my cap from my head. The solu-
tion was to go to the nearest tern-less pool pretending to myself
that I had quite finished fishing the other pool, so, a victory
for the brave birds.

There were many whimbrel, and cock golden plover in their
black decorative spring plumage adorned many hummocks.
Marauding skuas quartered the ground like enemy aircraft as
indeed they were to any young unsuspecting birds. The beautiful harlequins added colour to the rockier pools whilst dainty
phalaropes floated busily on the quieter pools with the same
fussy movements as their many wading cousins, scavenging for
flies. Greylags bred near the river whilst the cliff-nesting pink-
feet inhabited higher regions. Ever-gliding fulmars nested on the
ledges of the higher cliffs which dominated one side of the valley

— a long way from the sea. I met a young bird on the river and was told that they glide from the high cliffs, to as near the river as they can achieve and thence swim down some ten miles to join the others at the river mouth. I wonder how many or, more aptly, how few ever reach the ocean, with so many skuas, black-backs and ravens. These latter great birds attach themselves to the farms during the winter when all sheep must be in the sheds provided. The ravens become very tame and are regarded as pets, sometimes teasing the sheep dogs! Ptarmigan in some years were common and since the lichens and various berries grew at sea level these beautiful birds could be seen without the necessity of climbing to a thousand feet or more. With the approach of Autumn the leaves of the berries turn wonderful shades of red, and paint the landscape as with some artist's brush. A few trees grow in sheltered corners and gardens but dwarf willows of only a few feet grow beside the river as if fearing to be uprooted by the cold fierce winds, another example of nature's adaptability.

The most exciting fishings were the rocky pools below the foss. In order to reach the foss it was necessary to drive some six miles along a very rough track, then quite a hazardous

PHALAROPE

traverse where a bold bulldozer driver had carved a narrow path high on the hillside with the river far below. At one point the bulldozer had slid some way down; the driver and machine were only saved by the driver's skill. Eventually after some two miles of hair-raising journey a point of no-advance was reached in a boggy little meadow. This was only about a mile from the bottom of the beat but still a long, rough but exciting walk to the foss itself which could be seen afar as spray rose to a great height like mist. The foss pool was only approached from below by climbing down a steep slide with risk to rod and limb. The pool was most impressive, resembling the aisle of some great cathedral. The high walls were stained with surrealistic colours by the action of the water which ran down the walls drenching the fishermen on their approach, which necessitated wading in places on very slippery rocks. Here the salmon could be seen against the background of the cliffs and especially from above where every cast could be followed and every fishy movement seen – almost as exciting as the fishing itself. Playing a fish was most difficult in trying to avoid the great boulders. There was a narrow inlet to this cavern and below the river ran steeply through huge rocks as if some giant had hurled them, as children do with stones in puddles. An intrepid member of our party once followed a fish down to the next pool without breaking his rod, or his legs or indeed the cast. My nephew on one occasion slipped and broke his rod, and once mistook the route down to a pool and was only saved from serious injury by remembering what he had been taught at an Outward-Bound School – the lava rock face being most treacherous. My friend Bill, with whom I had gone to Norway, caught five fish in the Foss pool but realising that, as he had only one hand, he could not climb up the cliff with them, he constructed a small pool, by damming the exit with rocks, into which he put the fish as he caught them. When he had finished he removed the rocks and said a kind ''farewell'' to them as they swam away. He said later that he had grown quite fond of them.

THE FOSS POOL. RIVER HOFSA

I would not wish to leave Iceland without recounting the tale of a great fish which I hooked in a delightful pool called Simon's Island. I was fishing a method known as the Portland Creek Hitch and perhaps I should give a short account of this before I battle with the fish.

I read of the method in Lee Wulff's fascinating book *The Atlantic Salmon*. Sometime early in this century a British man o' war put into this harbour in Newfoundland. Finding that there were many salmon in the rivers, some officers found an old leather wallet in the Wardroom containing gut-eyed flies. When a fish was hooked the old gut-eyes broke but, being naval officers and therefore well trained in knots, they soon solved the problem with a half hitch round the shank. This caused the fly to "skate" and wobble in a most seductive manner and to the surprise of all, they caught the most fish. Thus was "the hitch" discovered and later adapted and improved by the ingenious Lee Wulff and others. This method on the shallow pools of Iceland proved most exciting and the fish so fresh from the sea perhaps thought that those objects skimming on the surface were some small fry endeavouring to escape.

On this particular occasion the fish were in receptive mood. I fished down the pool at first in the normal fashion and caught two, and then hitched with two half hitches on the side of the fly nearest the bank from which I was fishing and caught five more. At the third attempt a large fish hurled itself at the fly with a "plop" that I can still hear, and dashed madly round the pool in every direction. Finally when little backing remained, the line went slack. I waded out with little hope, clearing the line from rock to rock until suddenly a length of gut appeared, which I assumed was my own but as I lifted it I saw that the fly attached was not mine so there was still hope, and I continued my retrieving of the line, quartering the pool like a spaniel in search of a diving duck. There was still no sign of the line itself and finally the backing led me in my treasure hunt to the tail of the pool where the river divided at the Island's blunt and rocky head. The problem then was whether to take the high bank formed where floods of winter's melting snow and ice had piled giant stones and rocks for some five hundred yards, or to choose the left low bank on the island side. I perhaps foolishly, chose the high route thinking that I could more easily clear the line from the many rocks strewn below. This at first seemed the right decision, and after about fifty yards to my great joy, I felt the fish at long last which had rested behind a boulder where the line slackened. Before I had time to regain my breath he was away down the rapids, whilst I "came tumbling after"; thus I stumbled and slid until the river left the rapids at a left handed bend and a calm but short pool. I was still some fifty yards adrift at the end of the high bank when the fish reached a narrow spit of shingle before the next pool, and by exerting as much pressure as possible I managed to steer the fish up onto the distant shingle but, keeping on an even keel he waddled across the spit and back into the pool below like some amphibian.

Perhaps if I had slackened the line which was supporting him he might have fallen onto his side but I have often watched Icelandic fish ascend shallows when they are almost out of the water. The valley here is wide and flat and I then noticed that the wife of one of our party, having observed my antics, had approached on the far bank, but she told me afterwards that she was so astonished by the size of the great fish that she dared not cross in case she would be the cause of a disaster!

And so the struggle continued into a shallow pool where at last I drew level for the first time. The fish being now in such shallow water was understandably reluctant to come ashore and just when I thought I was at last the winner the fly came away and with a weary thrust of his great tail and swirl of waters the victor slowly swam away. He certainly deserved his freedom and I hope his progeny will return to enliven other fishermen who may be fortunate enough to visit those Elysian pools.

Perhaps I should guess his weight. Time does tend to exaggerate but remembering my friend Robin's great steelhead of which

I have written a rather disparaging account, I would none the less say that he too was over 30 lbs. A huge fish for Iceland and a most gallant opponent.

Having recounted my "hitching" experience, I must finish this chapter with my efforts to catch a salmon on a dry fly – a lifetime's ambition. I had failed on the Spey and Haffjardara but one fine hot day – all too rare as more often the cold winds blow down the valley from the frozen North – I decided to try again having read and re-read descriptions of how it should be done; the most hopeful ploy was to strike quickly which would suit me well since I could seldom restrain tightening if I rose a fish on a floating line. I knew that I should try to spot a fish first if possible so as to see by its movements whether it was likely to be interested. I soon saw a long shape and cast in front of it and at the sides many times with no response. I then remembered that I should try a cast well ahead so that the fish could have more time to watch the fly, so I cast some ten feet above, when it was instantly taken by a salmon and in my surprise I struck at once and so hooked and later landed my salmon. I then returned to see if my first fish was still there. It was, which was really not very surprising as it was a rock. I caught four more on that visit, one from a group of three in the foss pool which I could see clearly as I waded up behind a rock, and I can still see the fish in memory's film, as he rose slowly like a great trout to take my fly – of Lee Wulff type but resembling an angry wasp – instantly followed by a wild rush upstream as the reel sang its triumphant song.

Norway

Surely every salmon fisherman's ambition must be to visit Norway, a long held vision of deep fjords with mountains rising steeply from those depths towards the sky, the surface reflecting the great pine forests and pretty postcard villages, with perhaps an osprey or even the great white-tailed eagle soaring down in fishy quest. And, especially, the chance of an elusive leviathan in one of the great snow fed rivers which tumble and roar in a series of almost terrifying fosses down to those fjords.

So when my friend William Urmston suggested that I should join him to explore the rivers and lakes of Finmark, the most northern part of Norway and Finland – a land mostly inhabited by nomadic Laps and their reindeer, I was as excited as a small boy on his first fishing outing. William knew Norway well and was going out well in advance. He had a large American car which he loaded with every conceivable piece of fishing equipment including an inflatable rubber boat which perched on the roof, already blown up, so as to contain even more stores.

I was given careful instructions about what to bring and how to get there, essential for such an inefficient traveller. I was to fly up to an airstrip and then transfer to a tiny float plane for the last leg to Hammerfest where he would meet me.

Miraculously for once all went according to plan and my only difficulty was with a tin of worms for which I had an urgent signal from William, who is an "all-in" fisherman. Collecting them was a problem and the Customs quite rightly took a keen interest – perhaps they were fly fishermen. They consulted lists and they examined me as to what species they might be. As far as I can remember, having passed the Customs, they did not play an active part in William's fishing, being naturally almost moribund on arrival, since a tin must be a most unsatisfactory conveyance, even for a worm. The little otter float plane could not fly over the mountains, there being too much cloud, and anyway it had no head for heights, so we flew round the innumerable points low over the water.

I was much relieved to find William waiting as the narrow roads and sharp corners are most hazardous and the delightful Norwegians are at times rather thirsty and the laws were not then very strict. So we headed north, fishing where we could, by licence or approval, sometimes from the shore and sometimes from the boat, which was often very low in the water.

Our main objective was the great Tana river which flows north into the sea, not so very many miles from the Russian frontier, but where we were to fish, forming the boundary with Finland. William had arranged with the guest house where we were to stay that a boat would meet us at Karajok, a village where there was a school for Lapp children, with the idea that they should have a more sedentary life when they grew up. This little place was on a large tributary of the Tana into which it merged some twenty miles down stream.

We found the rendezvous place and indeed the boat, a large long canoe with high bow – but there was no sign of the navi-gator. This we later realised was not surprising, since when he eventually hove in sight he was weaving slightly from side to side. The Lapps wore their traditional dress of blue and red, with much red on their hats, particularly charming when worn by the cheerful children, and at times useful when in the thick birch forests for following one another. William could speak a little Norwegian, but the little Lapp seemed incapable of any coherent speech, and Lappish is a difficult language.

We stowed nearly all our fishing gear and belongings amid-ships whilst Bill and I sat side by side in the wide bows and the little Lapp stumbled unsteadily into the stern, and with some difficulty eventually started the outboard and we headed down river towards the junction with the Tana. Both rivers were mostly wide, and for the most part shallow with occasional hazardous rocks which we were told were sometimes moved by the melting spring ice, so that even experienced Lapps were at times wrecked and not long before our visit the local stores boat met such a fate. The river was fairly swift and we proceeded at a good speed as William and I admired the scenery. After about an hour the canoe suddenly altered course and we were speeding towards the bank. We looked round to find the little Lapp fast asleep with his head resting on the motor. We shouted but he could hear nothing and the canoe was too long for us to seize the helm. The bank was thickly wooded with many rocks but fortunately we struck at right angles, and benevolent fate selected a muddy patch up which the high bow rode as the boat quivered as an arrow striking a tree. The little Lapp woke from his slumbers, ran forward and shoved the boat back on course. If we had hit at an angle or struck rock or timber we would certainly have capsized into the very cold river with the loss of all our gear, the little Lapp – most Lapps cannot swim – and the boat. Even had we climbed ashore the struggle through the forest in a very sparsely populated area would have proved most unpleasant. However all was well but we kept a wary eye at every change of course.

Although mid-summer and light all night, when the sun set behind the mountains the air became very cold, and we were glad of the reindeer rugs which our future host had provided. The journey seemed interminable, especially as the outboard motor was continually breaking down, when we took to the oars, and once we stopped thankfully at a farm house where a kind farmer revived us with coffee. Eventually, after some nine hours we arrived at a farm of typical timber construction, run as a guest house, and were welcomed by the charming wife of a retired Norwegian Army Officer. We were cold and weary having completed the last part of the journey rowing, as the engine had finally faded altogether. The house overlooked the river.

The Tana is famous, especially because many years ago the local Lapp postman, whilst on his delivery, saw a large fish show, and trolled his spoon, which all boats carry, over the fish and hooked it. The post must have been even later than usual, since the fish when eventually landed, weighed 82 lbs, and is still the record Atlantic salmon. The postman's name was Henrik Henrikson and William had met him a few years before where he lived further down the river.

So we fished with great hopes of a "Storlak" as the largest salmon are known. I started before breakfast, fishing a large fly off the bank, and to my surprise, a good fish rose but missed and so I foolishly decided to rest it, and try again after breakfast. But when I returned, a Finn, who was staying in the house, and had evidently been watching from his bedroom window, was playing the fish, which he had hooked on the inevitable spoon, whilst I watched with mixed feelings. It was a most beautifully shaped fish of about 25 lbs.

William and I were keen to see the reindeer so when a Lappish girl appeared and we were told that she had come up river to try to find some of her mother's reindeer, which were thought to have wandered and joined another herd believed to be on the mountain tops some considerable distance from our guest house, we asked if we might accompany her.

We therefore followed her through the birch forest, where she was able to track the reindeer herdsman's progress by some means invisible to us. Each time she arrived at a stream she would sit down, take off her moccasins which were of reindeer hide but so that the upper half could be wound like putties around her legs. This was because her moccasins were filled with hay, thus forming comfortable insulation. Thus she crossed each stream barefooted, and so we proceeded somewhat laboriously, but in Lapland there is, as we had already learnt, no hurry. After many miles we began to climb, arriving eventually above the tree line. Thereafter we soon came on a place where they had camped, obvious even to us, since the ashes of the fire were surrounded by birch branches on which they had slept. Finally, after the sun had almost crossed the sky, we saw their tent with smoke curling from the top, wigwam fashion. The happy Lapps within were even happier when we entered the tent, and they roared with laughter. However, they made us welcome with much needed coffee and delicious reindeer meat fresh from a huge pan which hung above the fire. Around the fire sat the cheerful owner of the herd, her herdsman and innumerable dogs of every shape and size, and the herdsman of the girl's Mother who had taken the direct route over the mountains. Fortunately their reindeer were indeed there, identified by distinguishing clips from the ears. Reindeer are indeed beautiful, if rather ungainly animals, and these semi-domesticated herds move with unhurried grace, typical of life in that beautiful high country.

We wondered if future generations would find such happiness after their education to sedentary life. Later we asked our hostess on the river as to why they used such varieties of dogs, to which she replied "But they are all the same, with different fur."

When we were rested we thanked our hostess and especially the girl, our guide, as best we could and set off for home. We had a vague map, which like most maps, to me seemed to bear little, if any, resemblance to the landscape, especially as we had taken such a circuitous route through the forest, and had little idea as to even the approximate position of the camp. So we decided to head East and therefore eventually reach the Tana.

William had been severely injured in both legs in an accident which also cost him his right hand, but was in his determined way soon able to fish again, and with an ingenious ball joint to the oars, could row his boat, and even play and land a fish therefrom. But walking in such rough hilly country was most exhausting for him, and indeed for me. After wading across many streams and one quite wide river, and losing direction many times in the birch woods, we eventually arrived on the banks of the Tana. The problem then was whether the house was upstream or down. We opted for the latter and thankfully came at last to our destination.

The following day William was too exhausted to fish, so I went down to where I could wade out on a shallow and hooked what I thought was a trout and beached it. When I examined the fish it was literally a little old salmon of $2\frac{1}{4}$ lbs. So my dreams of a record salmon failed by a mere eighty pounds. I continued with the same rather large fly and caught another of $2\frac{1}{2}$ lbs – slightly nearer to that elusive record. I brought some scales home and they had spent four years in the river as parr and one winter in the sea.

The food was delicious, reindeer meat, salmon in all forms, Gravlax (dilled salmon) especially, and the delicious Multa or appropriately named cloud berries, blaeberries and many others.

But I still remember watching a Lapp in his canoe, trolling two large spoons and seeing him hook a fish, when he hastily pulled in the unsuccessful line, then picked up the other rod and stood amidships so that the boat swung broadside on to the current, and he hauled the unfortunate fish downstream with the weight of the boat, eventually gaffing it into the canoe. I still wonder how the postman hauled his leviathan downstream, but presumably the leviathan, when first hooked, pulled the postman upstream until, having failed to capture him or to break the incredibly strong line, the fish was dragged downstream.

Argentina and Uruguay

When I told an American friend that I was visiting South America in search of artists for my gallery, he told me that I must not leave there without meeting an Argentinian artist, Axel Amuchastegui. So when I was staying with an old friend in Uruguay we looked up the name in the Buenos Aires telephone book and amazingly found it. My friend's sister-in-law said that as she was going there the following day, she would call at the address. She telephoned in the evening to say that the artist had gone to Peru to visit Lake Titicaca high up in the Andes, and gave me his address in Lima. After visiting Patagonia I decided to return home via Lima where I met Axel for the first time, and as a result we had several exhibitions of this remarkable artist's work and eventually published *Some Birds and Mammals of South America.*

But I have again strayed from rivers. The Estancia which my friend managed was on a tributary of the River Plate. I borrowed an ancient spinning rod and reel, and as I left for the river my friend told me that I might meet some strange looking animals, looking like guinea pigs but the size of sheep. Knowing my friend's sense of humour I did not believe this until to my surprise I suddenly saw some of these extraordinary animals running into the reeds beside the river which is their home, and later swimming across. These Capybara are the largest rodents in the world. Unfortunately, although protected they are hunted for food and especially for their soft skins which make fine gloves. I caught only one small dorado, "the golden one" and a small fish which leapt into the boat via the back of my neck, which I took to be the voracious piranha which hunt in packs and can devour a sheep in a few minutes. However my host told me that it was only a fish known as "The toothy one".

There were many and wonderful varieties of birds including

70

the Screamers which resemble a cross between a goose and a crane but which, at times, unexpectedly soar uttering their strange cries.

And so to Argentina where a friend was to meet me off the ferry from which he whisked me, and after a mad dash, just caught the flight down to Bariloche. He had an introduction to Maurice Larivière, the owner of a beautiful estancia on the Traful river and had sent a telegram several days before. We drove along dusty roads, eventually crossing a ridge to reveal a very wide stony valley scoured by spring floods from the mountain snows, with the estancia house in the distance whilst the towering rugged peaks of the Andes formed an awe inspiring backdrop to the scene. As we neared the house we were aware of a figure reading a missive which proved to be our host reading our telegram! In spite of this lack of warning he made us most welcome and so we met his delightful wife and amusing family, for the first time. Here too I saw the giant condors which soared gracefully in the sky as if attached to the distant ground by lines, held by invisible boys, like kites.

The Traful river holds very large trout and "land-locked" salmon which latter had a most interesting origin. At the beginning of the century Americans decided to try to stock the river at Bariloche with these salmon from the State of Maine. The parr were brought down by ship to the nearest port on the south coast, over a thousand miles distant. Thence they were transferred to wagons and the tanks were no doubt refreshed with water from rivers en route. All went well until the fish on a hot day showed signs of distress, rising to the surface as they sought oxygen like goldfish in an overheated bowl. The American in charge of the operation decided very wisely, that it was useless to try to reach Bariloche with a lot of dead fish, and so as they happened to be crossing a beautiful clear river, released all the survivors into these refreshing and welcoming waters. This was the Traful not far from the confluence with a much larger river. The small parr were from land-locked salmon stock and so by instinct swam upstream, whereas their Atlantic salmon cousins would have drifted downstream. One can imagine the surprise and delight when some years later an unsuspecting trout fisherman hooked the first salmon.

At the head of the river is a beautiful lake, some ten or fifteen miles long, very clear, so that when I was there one could see a small forest which had slipped into the lake during one of the "quakes" which from time to time devastate this region – an impregnable retreat for trout or salmon!

The lake and river too are full of little crabs which must be the principal food of the fish. The salmon regard the lake as their "sea" and when they have the spawning urge drop down into the river so that the Top pool is the "sea pool" and is reserved

"LAND-LOCKED" SALMON

quite rightly for distinguished visitors like General Eisenhower. But below are many magnificent pools for lesser mortals where fish could be seen lying in Scottish indifference to our efforts, silhouetted by the bright sunshine against the shingle.

Now I have a friend in the Borders who rather fancies himself as a reader of scales, and so I took some scales home and sent them to him so that they arrived on the very first day of April. His conclusion was that the fish had spent two years in the river and a further two years in the sea! My subsequent "April Fool" telegram pointed out that the fish had never been within a thousand miles of the sea. As he seemed rather depressed I sent no more scales to him for some years when a further opportunity arose in the distorted shape of a hump-backed salmon of Russian origin which a friend caught whilst we were fishing in Iceland – a fish of some 3 lbs which looked as if it had accidentally been shut in a door. On that occasion he failed even to recognise the family salmonidae at all. Since then my friend for some reason refuses to read any scales for me.

Chile

Many years ago rainbow trout were introduced from North America into the fast-flowing clear rivers and deep lakes of Chile, fed from the melting snows of the Andes. They prospered, grew fat and multiplied and soon, inevitably, fishermen followed. I was on a business trip and for some reason found myself in Santiago with a rod and a few days to spare.

Patagonia, as most people will know, is the southern-most part of Argentina and Chile. Now the further south you travel the better is the fishing and the colder is the climate, with winds blowing incessantly from the Antarctic. This wild and beautiful country is indeed a paradise for fishermen, and for ornithologists, with incredible numbers and astonishing variety of birds from the flightless rheas and steamer ducks to the soaring giant condors.

I had hoped to fly down to Tierra del Fuego, "The uttermost part of the Earth", so well described by Bridges, the pioneer settler, in his book of that name, but had to be content with a flight to the lake district near the snow-capped volcano Villa Rica, with such liquid and appealing Indian names as Lake Llanqihue, Chinchuin and St Martine de Los Andes. The first evening I fished on one of the smaller lakes near the hotel catching two or three fish of two or three pounds. The following day we were to go down the river which flows from the lake.

I was told that the boatman would cook a trout in the dying embers of a fire, having first anointed it with oil and herbs, then wrapping it in wet paper. When the paper burns away, then the fish should be cooked to perfection and eaten, with a bottle of the excellent Chilean white wine.

Now it is a mistake to go fishing in Patagonia without learning Spanish and my kind niece had given me a gramophone record. Unfortunately this consisted of an extremely dull dialogue

74

between a Professor and a student, neither of whom were interested in fishing so that I soon became bored. Thus my Spanish consisted of only a few words such as the inevitable "Mañana" and "Claro" which I use when I do not understand a word of what is being said. I had also been taught some phrases in Buenos Aires, by the charming and excellent animal artist, Axel Amuchastegui.

We descended the river in a light but stable boat which the boatman propelled with skill at considerable speed. I soon found that such phrases as "Red at night shepherd's delight" which might have pleased the "pastores" were of little use in persuading the boatman to linger in slacker water where large expectant trout could be seen awaiting my fly. Other phrases such as "The last drop is the happy drop" and another concerning a camel were equally ineffective. Thus we proceeded apace down the river through magnificent country with glimpses of distant towering peaks of the Andes and through forests of Chilean beech (*Nothofagus*) now increasingly popular here. There was much bird life to be seen including Torrent Ducks, so truly named since they inhabit only the swift rapids, clinging to the rocks like the Copenhagen mermaid, sliding beneath the surface on our approach.

The sun rose higher in the sky, the time for that delicious meal came, and went, and at last the exasperated and exasperating boatman pulled ashore and produced a couple of large steaks which he grilled on a fire. Evidently he had seen me fishing on the previous evening and was taking no chances.

After our fishless lunch we set off again down the river at even greater speed. The country opened out and I saw an apparent giant fishing far out in the river. On rounding the bend, I saw that the fisherman was fishing from his horse using a long rod with no reel with his boy sitting behind him. As we passed, his son held up three fish to show us. I had nothing to show! The Chileans are wonderful horsemen and are said to be the origin of the Centaur legend. I was hoping that this particular centaur would hook a large fish and gallop downstream in pursuit.

The sun had now set behind the mountains. We had travelled many miles down the river and I was wondering how we were to get home. The boatman seemed in greater haste than ever and suddenly a road bridge appeared above us. We pulled ashore and there a lorry was waiting and our light boat was lifted aboard to join others which had evidently preceded us, which had carried sight-seers and not fishermen. There was a red sunset so that the "pastores" were "Contento" and, in spite of my lack of success, so was I.

CHILEAN FARMER AND HIS BOY

Antigua

For many years I have suffered at times from a most tiresome cough, which, as in Belloc's Cautionary Tale, concerning a certain Henry King "Physicians of the utmost fame" have failed to cure.

One winter when my cough had been especially tiresome, my kind nephew persuaded me to go with him to Antigua. Fishermen wherever they may be, grow restless if deprived of their sport for too long, so we consulted a local fisherman who agreed to take us out in his little fibre glass dinghy, and furthermore, reported that he knew where there was a monster barracuda which he had seen feeding voraciously on lesser fishes in a particular bay off the coral reef. He produced a small spinning rod, quite inadequate for the purpose, with no butt and of course no harness. The reel too was antiquated and he attached a weird sort of spoon to the steel trace.

Thus ill-equipped, we headed out through the reef and although Anthony had done some sea fishing in search of marlin, and my father had fished for tarpon and told us wondrous tales of those sporting fish, I did not expect to have inherited his skill, and was completely inexperienced in sea fishing. The sun was hot and the sea rather rough, and the boatman kept the outboard motor running which he deemed more practical and less exhausting than rowing. Anthony and I took turns at spinning, whilst the spoon landed with a great splash at varying distances and directions, but at least, except when we endangered each other, the ocean was a wide target and there were no obstacles such as trees which I had encountered when spinning in home waters.

We had been fishing for about an hour when the little rod was nearly pulled from my grasp and a huge fish jumped, sending a fountain of the clear Caribbean waters high in the air. The reel did not hold much line but we were able to follow the fish

with the engine. Anthony and the boatman identified the fish
as a barracuda, the tyrant of those warm coral seas, and probably
the very fish which the boatman had seen and sought. The struggle was long and as the rod had no butt, I had to hold it clear
of my body. Soon I started to cough with the effort and my arms
ached, and Anthony was convinced that the fish would win the
encounter, and no fisherman should ever hand over his rod until
"the strife is o'er the battle won . . ." I was absolutely exhausted
as the boat plunged in the choppy sea whilst my coughing fits
grew worse, but the great fish too was tiring and suddenly the
long sinister shape came alongside and for the first time, other
than his distant leaps, I could see him clearly like a huge thin
pike with a terrifying array of teeth like ill-fitting dentures. The
foolish boatman, instead of heading for the shore – which was
not too far distant – decided to try to lift the fish into the boat,
but in so doing touched the propeller and with a sickening twang
the steel trace was severed. The fish was far too heavy and indeed
too large even to attempt to bring aboard.

This was almost my first and nearly my last sea fishing experience, and my first sight of one of those piratical fish, so I am
no judge of their size. Billy Flynn, the Blackwater ghillie, on

being asked the size of a huge fish – later thought to be a vast "poike" which had turned from a bait at the last moment – replied "Sure 'twas as long as a boat and half as long as a rod". My fish was as long as our boat and the biggest the boatman had ever seen – beginner's ill-luck! Anthony is still convinced that it must have been the Caribbean record.

I soon recovered and hope that the barracuda is now also "half as long as a rod"! He had indeed fought well even if his opponent was rather incapacitated.

Now I believe that I have found a cure for my affliction and although perhaps out of place in a book supposedly on fishing, none the less even fishermen have coughs and might be interested, and even amused by the accidental discovery of my cure.

I am a most inexpert keeper of bees, and one day last spring David Creese, our neighbour's gamekeeper, reported a swarm on one of my little apple trees. I had never taken a swarm but thought I knew what I should do and David's father had been a bee-keeper, so David proffered advice from a safe distance having no veil. I collected my veil, gloves, a box and blanket and advanced tentatively on the swarm. The first part of the operation went surprisingly well, the swarm fell into the box which I covered carefully with the blanket and put near the hive. I then put a ramp covered with a sheet leading to the hive's entrance and retired to await the coming of dusk.

When I returned after some confidence-building refreshment, I emptied the box with a flourish of the blanket with the panache of a bullfighter's cloak, or the twirl of a magician's as he triumphantly causes his beautiful accomplice to vanish wastefully into thin air. But my own effort was to ensure that no bees remained in box or blanket – and so it was, as all had found an escape route worthy of Colditz!

Two friends arrived to stay that evening, Raoul Millais, the distinguished painter of horses, and Bobby Wills, who could be relied on to contribute to the amusement or chaos. I told them of my swarm and Bobby uncharacteristically rose before breakfast to search for the swarm, which I secretly hoped had departed to a quieter haven. However Bobby reported at breakfast that he had located the swarm, about 20 feet up in a crab-apple tree. David Creese passed my door each morning and said that all I had to do was to put the blanket under the swarm, cut off the branch with a long scissored pole which I possess, and put the box over the Queen – very good in theory, but in practice the bough struck a lower branch and the swarm dispersed angrily in every, but mostly in my direction. I fled into the neighbouring dog-wood. The swarm followed their queen faithfully into another high branch when exactly the same "aggro" (to use a modern expression) happened, except that the bees were even more militant!

I then remembered that a neighbour, Ronny Hay, was an expert apiarist and furthermore had been in the Navy and was thus most qualified for climbing masts or trees. He arrived within the hour complete with box, ladder, smoke, veil, gloves and all the other necessary regalia for queen catching. He climbed his ladder but we had pruned so many branches that he could not reach the swarm which was then on a slender bough. So he told me to stand immediately under the swarm so that he might climb up the ladder which I held perpendicularly, and cut off the branch which he would then carry down and put branch and swarm into the box. Unfortunately the secateurs were blunt so that at intervals a shower of angry bees fell on my head. Eventually he severed the bough and carried the swarm past my nose down the now trembling ladder, and placed it in the box, covering it nautical fashion with a tarpaulin. We retired for further refreshment and Ronny, when he left, told us to wait until dusk before "hiving the swarm".

When the time came I press-ganged Bobby into holding one end of a board on which we placed the box and carried it as on a stretcher and put it inside the hive so that the bees could sort themselves out. The undergrowth leading to the hive was very thick and Bobby, who was unprotected, protested volubly.

However the sailor's knots around the tarpaulin held, and we accomplished our task at last as darkness fell. Which at long last brings me to the point of the story. When I took off my gloves a bee, which had been waiting for just such an opportunity, stung the palm of my hand which began to swell. When the swelling reached my wrist watch and tightened under the strap, I remembered that I had been given some little pills called Piriton, and surprisingly found them. The swelling went down almost immediately and the horrible cough which had bothered me for weeks vanished overnight!

I doubt whether it is necessary to annoy a bee, before taking the pill, in order to achieve a cure!

Australia

TASMANIA:

The Casting Vote

In election year, I was reminded of a somewhat unusual but effective electioneering ploy. I was on a visit to the beautiful island of Tasmania with a friend on behalf of the Fairbridge Society. We were staying with our chairman, General Wordsworth, who was a keen fisherman. So when we had a spare day he took me into the wild hilly country to try for a trout in a little river very overgrown, beneath huge gum trees.

I never fully enjoy fishing rivers where the banks are shorn like well kept lawns, and get far more pleasure, if less fish, from natural rivers with wild fish – although obviously originally introduced probably from North American stock. Kenya is an example where early British settlers went to immense trouble, resulting for a time in enormous trout which were eventually poached with dynamite and suchlike methods of destruction. I had a most enjoyable day's fishing in the Aberdare Mountains, but found the unusual hazards of keeping an eye out for lions, buffaloes, crocodiles and especially hippos, made concentration difficult.

In Tasmania there were no such hazards or distractions as we waded or more often, scrambled up the little river, the banks being virtually impassable. A few trout rose, usually in impregnable positions beneath trees or behind rocks, as is their wont. The day was hot and so was I, and my host suggested a rest on the bank below a footbridge high above the river.

"Wordy", for such was my host known to all, told me that he had stood for the senate the previous year, and not being really a politician, he had become exasperated with electioneering, so that instead of attending the eve of the poll meetings he had decided to go fishing instead, and came to this remote and peaceful river, as he thought, far from the electioneering scene. There was a good trout rising under the overhanging tree just below the bridge – a very awkward cast, but eventually the fly avoided the clutching branches and alighted in front of the trout which rose, was hooked, and eventually landed after a good fight. Wordy carried the fish up the path to the footbridge above when he became aware of a figure leaning on the footbridge. The man came up to him and asked his name. "Wordsworth" was the reply. "Are you the bloke who is standing for the senate in tomorrow's elections?" When Wordy said "I am", the bloke replied "Well anyone who can catch a fish like that is certainly worth my vote – I'll vote for you!"

I would like to record that he was elected by this casting vote, but the truth is that he was such a popular character that he had a good majority, and also a fine trout for supper.

*   *   *

My other excursion was to The Great Lake, where at one time near the dam, at a certain month had a famous "rise", somewhat similar to our Mayfly, but of I think a sedge-like fly which excited fish and fishermen alike. Sadly, the height of the dam had been raised which had the dual affect of destroying the ''rise'' and almost all the trees at the lake's edge so that I was met with the depressing sight of, as it were, a petrified forest. As I had no boat I waded through the dead wood, peering around the trees as if stalking aquatic rabbits. After about an hour I became aware of a strange rather square object with twigs at each corner, which resembled a log, which I was sure had not been there a moment before. I stood still and watched and the little creature dived, then surfaced again a few yards away. I then saw that it was that improbable egg-laying mammal, a Duck-Billed Platypus. (Although I caught no fish, I count that day as one of my most memorable.) Evidently they consider that they are less obvious to hawks if they remain still on the surface unlike our water voles which seem to enjoy crossing and re-crossing a river, like ferry boats.

DUCK-BILLED PLATYPUS

We heard that two members of the Walt Disney Studios were filming the weird and wonderful birds and mammals of Australia and called at the village where they were working. They were a charming couple called Mallot, who were living in the bungalow of a bushman named Mot Turner. Mrs Turner told us that her husband was dedicated to animals and used to "go walk-about" returning at intervals to earn sufficient for the family, so life had been hard until the arrival of the Mallots who had heard of her husband's extraordinary affinity with animals. Apart from many marsupials, most Australian animals are nocturnal, so they had to be caught to be filmed – against the Mallots' normal practice – in semi-artificial conditions. For this purpose Mot Turner had caught a great variety which were housed in sheds and pens in their garden.

The Mallots said that Turner had an amazing knowledge and way with animals so that he tamed them in a very short time; that he had always wanted a monkey, so they had given him one "and they get along very well". It was indeed very beautiful and intelligent. Mr Turner then showed us round his menagerie stopping occasionally to thrust his hands into the straw, producing like a conjurer, amazing creatures, like wombats in three sizes, Granpa Wombat being very portly. There were Tasmanian Devils and at one shed an animal which he said was very fierce, a sort of wild cat but more in the form of a large mongoose. He pretended that he was scared of it and then cuddled it in his arms and tickled its tummy!

Sadly the Tasmanian Tiger, a stripey dog-like beast which had inhabited the almost impenetrable horizontal bush country, was thought to be extinct but I have recently read that it has now been seen in Western Australia where it was previously unknown, so perhaps the Tasmanian Tiger will reappear.

Mrs Turner told us that the Disney organisation had been most kind to them and that their future was assured but no doubt Mot Turner continued to "go walk-about" at times, and I believe that a small zoo was established under their care.

VICTORIA :

Delatite

My only fishing on the mainland of Australia was in the State of Victoria. My niece who lives in Melbourne, took me to stay in the hills about two hours drive, on the beautiful property of Delatite, with a lovely garden in the English style. A delightful little river flowed at the bottom of the garden, and Mark, the son of our kind hosts, took me down to fish. I was warned to beware of Tiger snakes which haunted the roots and rocky banks, but these were soon forgotten as I tried, not very successfully, for the trout.

My most abiding memory was hearing a strange thumping noise approaching from behind. I appreciated that Tiger snakes slithered rather than thumped and turned to see a kangaroo approaching, which came right up to us and stood like a ghillie to watch. Mark explained that it had been reared by hand as a 'Roo at the neighbouring farm and when it had nothing better to do, often came down to see how he was getting along. A delightful interlude.

On our way up, Charles McCubbin the Australian artist, naturalist, and broadcaster, had taken us to a forest reserve. We were wandering along a track when a bird called. Charles asked us if we knew what it was and then explained that it was a Lyre Bird imitating another bird. We stopped to listen and in a short time the Lyre Bird had given us a concert of its full repertoire. He wrote down for me their names : Yellow Backed Cockatoo, Crimson Rosella, Grey Thrush, Yellow Wattle Bird, Golden Whistler, Rufous Whistler, White-browed Scrub Wren, Kookaburra, Pied Currawong, Eastern Whip bird. He told us that in another part of the forest near a bend in a road, lived another Lyre Bird which could imitate the screech of tyres of a car taking the corner too fast, which luckily could not be used as evidence against the driver.

LYRE BIRD

We crept nearer to our Lyre bird and watched him displaying and running in a figure of eight where he had beaten down a track by his strange antics. Perhaps the most amazing bird that I have ever seen and heard, revealed to us by Charles McCubbin's knowledge in the Acheron Way forest.

Altogether we saw at Delatite thirty-two different species of birds, including a juvenile Pallid Cuckoo being fed by its foster parents, Yellow-faced Honey-eaters, Sacred Kingfishers, Dusky Wood Swallows, the Willy Wagtails, Sulphur Crested Cockatoos, Kookaburras – which are dry kingfishers – the delightful Blue Fairy Wrens, Wedge Tailed Eagles and Goshawks.

New Zealand

The Aunt's Net, and the Huya Bird

All fishermen long for the chance to fish in New Zealand. My opportunity came when I was to visit a gallery in Auckland. I told this to a friend in the Flyfishers' Club who said that he had an Aunt out there where he kept a landing net – an essential piece of equipment where the fish are large. Furthermore he telephoned that evening to farmer friends in the South Island who most kindly offered to put me up for a few days. I seldom fly anywhere without a rod, so plans were unexpectedly soon complete.

A few days later, having completed my business in Auckland, I flew down to Gore in the South Island armed with the Aunt's net and a licence which, for a small sum, entitled me to fish many rivers in that particular area. I hired a rather doubtful looking motor car and eventually found my way to the farm where I was made most welcome by the family.

The country there is rather flat with heavily wooded hills rising steeply, whilst the fat sheep and cattle testified to the richness of the pastures. The woods were full of the most enormous red deer which sadly are regarded as vermin, and at that time were often shot from helicopters. A young man staying at the farm was a skilled stalker, and surely there are many sportsmen who would enjoy stalking amongst those fine hills with the chance of shooting a beast with a head undreamed of in Scotland, and with knowledgeable guides, the deer population could perhaps be thus properly controlled.

I chose to fish a couple of nearby quiet dry fly rivers, rather overgrown in places but this only adds to the enjoyment. I returned one evening and proudly produced a beautiful trout of some 2 lbs. Then the young man of the house took me to the lawn where lay the most enormous eel, some four or five feet long, caught in the local creek. The method would not perhaps have found favour with the purists as it consisted of lowering a piece of meat on strong line into a deep hole, and when the eel took the bait, to pull it if possible sufficiently clear of its lair and then spear it with a trident of which Neptune himself would have been proud.

I was reminded of an occasion many years before, when I went into the delightful Ogden Smiths, at the Sign of the Golden Hooks in St. James's Street, and was examining some tiny 000 dry flies when a much more enterprising sea angler appeared and bought a huge hook, which in itself must have weighed a couple of pounds, with which he hoped to catch an enormous conger. I was rather envious until I asked him how he would kill it – "Chop its head off with my axe" he replied. I had visions of the boat sinking and of the occupants being devoured by the leviathan's hungry and angry relations.

There were many fascinating birds but for once I did not have a bird book, but even if out of context, I must tell the sad tale of the Huya bird as told me by my friend the distinguished New Zealander, Raymond Ching, who has portrayed the beautiful Kiri Te Kanawa with the facility with which he paints Kiwis and other fascinating birds.

The Huya bird is a sacred bird of Maori Chiefs whose head-dresses are decorated with the beautiful tail feathers, and for this reason the birds are afforded protection. The curious feature of these birds is that the male has a comparatively short pointed beak, whereas the lady Huya has a long slender curved bill – nature ordained that the male should enlarge the holes of grubs in decaying wood, when the lady Huya would insert her dainty bill and remove the succulent grub.

The Huya birds are now thought to be extinct. Could it be that the greed of the lady Huyas caused starvation to their hard working husbands rather than any suspicion of the head-dresses of Maori Chiefs? I feel sure that neither are to blame.

Raymond Ching and some friends were determined to find

out if any Huyas survived, so when he heard of a bushman who had recently seen a pair, he took the train to the nearest station and eventually met the bushman, who told him that he had watched a pair at the top of a pollarded willow feasting on snails as in a Parisian restaurant, and offered Raymond one of the shells from which the Huyas had extracted the snail. Raymond took out a match box and put the shell, wrapped in cotton wool, carefully in his pocket, and in great excitement set off for home in the train. Now Raymond is, or certainly was, a chain-smoker, so when he decided that he must smoke he put a cigarette in his mouth, took the match box from his pocket, shook it, and, when it did not rattle, threw it from the window. He had arranged for the other Huya enthusiasts to come round so that he could recount what the bushman had told him. ''And now'', he said proudly, ''I will show you a shell from which a Huya

89

extracted a snail". He put his hand in his pocket and then, and only then, did he realise what he had done! The loss of some great fish is as nothing to the loss of that little snail shell!

Raymond gave me a book on the Huya and in an envelope a tail feather!

But as usual I have strayed and as usual have left little time to catch the aeroplane, and as I came in sight of the airport buildings, there was a loud bang and I saw in my mirror, a large lump of car bounding along the road before leaping into the nearside ditch. I had no time to stop, but when I admitted the loss of their precious part, the good lady in charge was quite unperturbed.

As for the Aunt's net, I returned this rather apologetically, as I thought that a more skilled fisherman would have made better use of it, but after all in the Irishman's definition "a net is just a lot of holes tied together with string"!

'Beautiful British Columbia' and 'Radar'

A good friend, and oft times fishing companion, asked me to go to join a party organised by his son who was then working in New York.

I had for many years hoped to fish for Steelheads – a species of migratory rainbow – ever since I bought a stiff ten foot rod made by Hardy's especially designed for such powerful fish, but which I used in the summer on the Frome in Dorset for salmon. The rod was called the Rogue River which I learned was a steelhead haunt.

So we flew, at first in a Jumbo to Vancouver where we joined our American contingent and headed north in diminishing-sized planes. The last lap was in a small aeroplane into which we only just fitted, and flying at lower altitudes were able to admire the colours of the Fall, especially the golden hued cottonwood trees and other poplars and the many lakes and rivers, and earlier in our flight, the magnificence of the Rockies.

We finally landed on a landing strip cut in some firs which looked most hazardous as we approached. This was on the edge of the Bear River and in the pool below, we could see the remains of dead King Salmon which had spawned already and died, to become the feast of Bald Eagles which rose at our approach, and at night they became supper for the bears. The Bear Lake and Bear River flow into the Skeena.

Anticipation plays an enormous part in any fishing expedition, and our journey was the perfect prelude on this occasion, as the wind in the trees blended harmoniously with the music of our river below us.

As we stood in admiration of such sights and sounds we heard a helicopter approach which settled gracefully. A lean weather-beaten looking character stepped from the machine. We learned later that he was known as ''Radar'' – real name Patrick O'Reilly.

A keen fisherman and naturalist who was often employed by the Canadian authorities to monitor the herds of caribou which he adored. We were told that on one occasion he had knocked a wolf from a ledge with the skid of his plane, which was threatening to do the same to a young caribou. Certainly he was a most skilled pilot in that difficult rugged country.

Thus we made our final approach of only a few minutes duration down river with our noses pressed against the windows, peering at the fast rocky pools which rushed past, and we landed in a welcoming shower of golden leaves which the downdraught had sent soaring upwards towards the poplars from which they had so recently fallen. Here we were met by Floyd Boyd, the head guide, who had great knowledge of the wilderness around, being a trapper in winter.

The Camp consisted of a log cabin, where we ate our very good meals, prepared by the wife of one of the guides, and where we gathered each evening to recount our various adventures and misadventures over a glass of whisky before dinner, at the American well named "happy hour". We slept in tents with wooden floor boards and a stove, but the dry birch logs burnt so quickly that on more than one occasion during the nights, I relighted the stove, since winter was already dusting the mountains with snow. One of our party even took the temperature within his tent with a thermometer from his fishing bag, which already registered freezing point.

A splendid dog resembling the ridge-back lion dogs, slept beneath the log cabin and kept marauding scavenging bears away.

Behind the camp a perpetual plume of smoke signalled the fish smoker. The fish were cut into strips and laid on grills and were delicious, eaten each evening as we gathered before supper.

As the poplars had donned their winter plumage, so had the "buck" Steelheads assumed their astonishing spawning colour of royal-red. By then the geese had departed south with their young, so that their wild calls would not be heard again before

BALD EAGLE

heralding the coming of spring. Bald Eagles remained to scavenge with the bears on salmon kelts, and later on, animals weak from age or injury, and slain by a remorseless northern winter. One day I watched two moose wade across the river. I tried to film them but I was in a boat and was so thrilled by their vast size, that my efforts became known as the "Wobbly Moose film". One day we met a porcupine, which to our surprise climbed up a tree. Our guide told us that they were protected as they can easily be killed with a stick and thus provide meat for any starving tracker lost in that remote wilderness. Our guide always carried a rifle in case a grizzly should become aggressive if separated from her cubs, or in a bad temper, being rather unpredictable. Two of our party were fishing about a mile above the lodge, when their guide espied what he thought was a log coming down the river. When the log landed and stood up he realised that it was a grizzly and shouted to the fishermen, who, in the words of one of them showed "a sudden attachment" to the boat. Luckily the engine started as the great bear approached. They said afterwards, that they were not so much frightened by the bear, which probably had no evil intent, but by the reputation of the guide, who was said to be a very bad shot!

GRIZZLY

And so at last to the fishing. We set out each day to our allotted pools in jet boats, which are propelled by water power, sending plumes of water in their wake, and rising high as they went over the rocky shallows, which with the usual outboards, would have often damaged the propellers. The river was in places strewn with trees, felled by industrious beavers.

In the late Fall the fish lie deep in the pools, so that we fished with sinking lines, and allowed the heavily dressed flies to come round slowly. We were allowed to kill only two fish each per day, which was quite sufficient for our needs and indeed, one of our party – a charming Texan, and a wonderful fisherman with a small light rod, returned all his fish. He belonged to the Recycling Club, whose members help to assure the future of these and other splendid fish. At times we caught a species of char called Dolly Vardens. These were not very sporting fish, nor very good to eat, so the guides left them on the shore for the bears.

The Steelhead did indeed live up to their reputation, being very strong jumpers, many times and broke our tackle on several occasions round huge rocks and submerged branches. Our Texan friend, Fred Harrison, had a great fight with a large "buck" which got round a rock in midstream. He waded out very deep and eventually freed the line, when the fish did a huge jump in a flurry of spray. When he eventually landed it, he carried it in his arms like a fat scarlet baby to release it, and I have a photograph of that good sportsman so doing.

My friend Robin also hooked a very large fish which encounter I tried to film. When the fish eventually escaped I think he was more annoyed that I had run out of film, or in any case was not looking when it too did a great jump which would have confirmed its vast size, than with the actual loss of his fish. Fred's fish must have exceeded 20 lbs so how large was Robin's? His fish grows each year like many others, with the telling, and must now be nearly 30 lbs, as perhaps it was? Robin is a most skilful photographer and later gave me an album of wonderful mementoes.

One of our party was summoned by his company to attend a conference, but quite rightly, refused to do so unless they would fly him out and back, so as to lose as little as possible of his hard-earned fishing holiday. The redoubtable "Radar" arrived and a couple of days later returned with him after a successful meeting. "Radar" then offered to fly some of us down to the junction with a larger river, the Skeena. We landed beside the pool and went our various ways, whilst Radar produced a telescopic spinning rod and soon hooked and landed a fine buck steelhead of some 16 lbs. So, as dusk fell, we climbed aboard with one or two lesser fish, and flew back in triumph to show the others Radar's well deserved catch, and soon after he flew off with it, back to his house in the hills and to his supper.

And so, after a warning snowfall, even at our camp's level, we too departed after a splendid holiday, being so well looked after by our guides, so well fed by their wives, and with gratitude to our host, who had each evening taped our rather reluctant experiences during "the happy hours" which he later sent over to us. So we can be reminded of these events, and my "Wobbly Moose" film does include pictures of our camp, the guides, the redoubtable Radar, and some even wobblier Bald Eagles, but Robin's photographs are certainly the best record of "beautiful British Columbia", in the words of our host.

Anyone whose interest in Steelheads may have been sparked by my description of fishing for these most sporting fish, should certainly read one of the books by Roderick Haig-Brown, that great writer and fisherman. I have recently re-read *A River Never Sleeps*. He caught his first salmon on our humble little Frome, and later emigrated to Vancouver, and from there fished most of the great Steelhead rivers of the West Coast. His descriptive powers enable the reader to follow the thrills of winter fishing, and certainly to learn much of the skill and endurance required. John Ashley-Cooper also caught his first salmon on the Frome, and became perhaps our greatest salmon fisherman and a masterly writer of "salmon" books.

Concluding Thoughts

EVOLUTION OF THE SALMON

When I began to write this book I had intended to include stories of events which were of interest or amusing, but in recording these, which brought back memories over a long period and in many rivers, I thought that perhaps I might be excused for ending with changes which seem to have occurred concerning salmon fishing methods and the noble salmon themselves.

I have myself always enjoyed trying new ideas, either from books read, or from expert fishermen. During my life, fishing near the surface with the then greased line became the vogue, developed especially by Arthur Wood on the Aberdeenshire Dee. Formerly silk-worm gut was used, which most will know, had to be soaked overnight. Jack Mills of Bisterne, on our Avon, told me the sad tale of a great fish which he saw in the tail of one of his pools – he had no time to go back for his rod that evening and forgot to soak his cast. So the next morning he started at the top of this long pool, thinking that by the time he reached the tail, the cast would have soaked sufficiently. The fish had moved up to the neck during the night, took his fly at once, and broke him. It was caught a month or two later further upstream and weighed nearly fifty pounds.

On the subject of gut, Miss Ratcliffe, my mentor, used to tell me to "curtsy the rod" as a hooked fish jumped lest it should fall back on the brittle cast, but I now believe that with nylon it is better to keep the line taut, since nylon is so elastic and to slacken the line often frees the hook. I hooked a bramble one day, pulled as hard as I could when the double hooked fly catapulted into the very corner of my eye, but luckily one of the hooks lodged against the bone at the eye's edge.

But are salmon changing their habits? When I first read Gilbert's *Tale of a Wye Fisherman* I was fascinated to read that the master Robert Pashley, caught the majority of his many salmon with an ancient rod, stripping in the fly by hand as fast as possible. I tried this on my next visit to the Frome and rose ten fish. I did not land many, being a novice at this method, but improved later on. Now I seldom rise ten in a season there, and find myself increasingly inept on other rivers as well, even when pools seem full of fish, and this year in particular, my friends, for the most part, tell the same tale, even when conditions seem good.

On our beat on the Frome many fish move up about the month of November when they are in full spawning livery matching the autumn tints. Where had they been hiding? The owner of the lowest beat on the river, where few fish had been seen or caught in recent seasons, asked the Wessex Water Authority to investigate. They were employing Peter Fox to monitor the movement of salmon of all ages. He therefore took the electric fishing apparatus down, and to everyone's astonishment recorded over four hundred salmon and some three hundred sea trout! How sensible of the salmon to remain there until spawning time – probably safer than the perils of the sea.

The Freshwater Biological Association has a laboratory just below us, doing so much interesting work. They also operate a fish counter, and my neighbour, David Rasch, once played the only fish which had run, for the length of the meeting of our local Association, it eventually escaped under the Bunny!

I asked a most knowledgeable scientist there how we could account for the fish remaining each year concealed in that deep lowest beat. "Oh" he said "Evolution!"

I wonder whether the increasing reluctance of fish to take my fly can be attributed to the same cause, or just to me? It is obvious that free-taking fish are less likely to reach their spawning beds, could it be that the majority of the ova are spawned by the fish which have plagued us during the previous season by ignoring even the most beautiful flies offered in whatever sizes and colours and that the fish which eventually return from the sea will inherit these same habits? Let us hope not!

Epilogue

This book began with my native Avon, which was never far from my thoughts on my travels, and so I will conclude with my home, Kingfisher Mill, astride the Avon, the true *Quiet Waters* of my title. As I write, now in Autumn, the eels will be migrating down river to their distant spawning area in the Sargasso sea, passing the salmon moving up river to the gravel shallows of the upper Avon and a few pairs will soon be here.

Migration is a constant source of wonderment. Whilst our salmon and eels travel vast distances, thankfully our trout remain. Here on the Avon the Piscatorial Society's policy of encouraging wild trout is succeeding well, and our beautiful native fish, distinguished by a few large red spots, are again becoming more numerous each season.

A friend, a good fisherman, especially amongst trees on the Bristol Avon near his home, came over to fish at the very end of the season. So I took him in the evening to fish the Mill Pool where several good trout were rising – an awkward cast through a narrow gap. I told him of my great nephew Charles's incantation, so he said to the largest trout "I am cleverer than you trout and I'm going to catch you" but then added "because you're a silly trout". Now you must always treat your fish with the greatest respect, and so the spell was broken and the fly on his back cast deservedly lodged firmly in a willow. I went to the Mill, only a few yards away, to fetch a long pole, most cunningly devised, for such occasions, and lopped the offending branch, returning on four occasions to lop further branches!

Now the season is over and my cherry trees have donned the colours of the "Buck" Steelhead of British Columbia, and as my dog Drake walked me along the footpath a chill wind from the north-east blew through the new gap, as a further reminder of the coming of winter. I glanced at the pool and thought that I heard a chortle from the big trout, and there he was, enjoying a final "sherry" (spinner) and the last laugh. Let us hope that this trout, whose name is Augustus, will end in Rupert Brooke's Heaven where:

'Oh! never fly conceals a hook
Fish say, in the Eternal Brook'